Monetary Mindfulness

for High School Students

Dr. Angela K. Love

Angela K. Love
P.O. Box 452
Campbell, TX 75422

Previously published December 2016 as *Personal Finance: A Working Textbook*.
Previous published ISBN: 978-0-9978407-0-4

Cover design and interior financial icons by Lisa Kerner of Designs by Lisa Kerner

illustrations by Angela K. Love unless otherwise stated.

Professional editing provided by Barbara McKibbin.

Reach us on the Internet: www.angelakayelove.com

ISBN: 978-1-7342305-2-9

INTRODUCTION

Teens who learn money management skills in high school make better money decisions in adulthood. However, much of the curriculum available for teens lacks a comprehensive review of money concepts. This textbook fills that gap.

Course Structure:

- 46 Lessons
- 12 Sections
- 10 Quizzes
- 2 Unit Tests
- 1 Final Comprehensive Exam

Course Benefits:

- Self-Paced Learning: Your teen will start with the basics to ensure they understand more complicated money topics.
- Math Credit: This course fulfills a one-year math credit requirement. Your teen will learn math formulas and ratios related to money management, and financial concepts and terms.
- Confidence Building: By the end of this course, students will be confident in basic money management skills, which they can use professionally and personally.

The answer key for this textbook, Monetary Mindfulness for High School Students Answer Key, is available for purchase separately. You can find it where this textbook is sold.

LEARNING OBJECTIVES

Upon successful completion of this course, students will be able to do the following:

Unit 1

- Identify types of income.
- Explain the three types of expenses.
- Understand ways to save money.
- Describe the ways people give.
- Differentiate between assets and liabilities.
- Classify assets into short or long-term.
- Classify liabilities into short-term, long-term, or contingent.
- Complete a personal financial statement.
- Explain the difference between gross and net wages.
- Understand types of wage withholdings.

Unit 2

- Apply basic financial theories to everyday financial decisions.
- Differentiate between financial account types.
- Know how to open a checking and savings account.
- Reconcile a checking and savings account.
- Write a check.
- Explain types of investment tools.
- Differentiate between stocks, bonds, mutual funds, and other investments.
- Distinguish between a secured loan from an unsecured loan.
- Calculate a loan payment.
- Describe a creditor's loan approval process.
- Read and understand a credit report.
- Explain the components of a FICO Score.

Unit 3

- Identify financial pitfalls.
- Describe healthy financial habits.
- Create a budget.
- Manage a budget.

TABLE OF CONTENTS

UNIT I
FINANCIAL CONCEPTS

Learning Objectives

Upon successful completion of this unit, you will be able to do the following:

- Identify types of income.
- Explain the three types of expenses.
- Understand ways to save money.
- Describe the ways people give.
- Differentiate between assets and liabilities.
- Classify assets into short or long-term.
- Classify liabilities into short-term, long-term, or contingent.
- Complete a personal financial statement.
- Explain the difference between gross and net wages.
- Understand types of wage withholdings.

SECTION 1 - INCOME AND EXPENSES

KEYWORDS

Discretionary expenses
Dividend rate
Early withdrawal penalty
Fixed expenses
In-kind
Internal Revenue Service
Laddering
Net income
Passive income
Revenue
Shares
Shareholders
Unearned income
Dividend
Diversifying
Earned income
Giving
Interest rates
Itemizing
Maturity date
Net Profit
Personal income
Savings
Share accounts
Tax liability
Variable expenses

LEARNING OBJECTIVES FOR SECTION 1

Upon successful completion of Section 1, you will be able to:

- Identify types of income.
- Explain the three types of expenses.
- Understand ways to save money.
- Describe ways people give.

LESSON 1 - INCOME

Monthly Business Income

Revenues	$30,000
Expenses	28,500
Net income	$1,500

Monthly Personal Income

Income	$3,000
Giving	300
Savings	300
Expenses	2,400
Breakeven	$0

The term *income* is often used interchangeably with the term *revenue*; however, the two terms have different meanings. **Revenue** is used by companies on their financial statements. In general terms, revenue is the cash earned for goods and services before expenses are paid. Money earned by companies through investments is not considered revenue unless investments are part of their main business venture. For companies, income is the money left after all expenses have been paid and other income has been added. Income after expenses is usually referred to as **net income** or **net profit**.

Money earned by individuals, such as yourself, is referred to as personal income rather than revenue. **Personal income** is money that is received for performing work, providing services, owning investments, or other sources such as child support. Income is referred to as either earned income or unearned income. All income is taxable by the **Internal Revenue Service** (IRS). The exception to this is income received from others living in the same house for performing activities such as babysitting siblings, mowing the lawn, or receiving an allowance for completing chores. While this money is a form of income, the IRS does not require taxes to be paid on it.

The IRS is the revenue service for the federal government of the United States. The IRS is a bureau of the Department of the Treasury. The IRS collects revenue from assessed taxes on the earned and unearned income of people and businesses. The IRS is also responsible for enforcing the tax laws in the U.S.

Earned income is money received for performing work or providing services. It can be in the form of cash or an in-kind object. An **in-kind** payment is made when a person receives an item in exchange for work performed such as receiving room and board for providing cleaning and childcare services. In-kind payments are considered to be of equal value as the work performed. In-kind payments are subject to federal income taxes and taxable in states where income is taxable.

Personal income is money that is received for performing work and/or services.

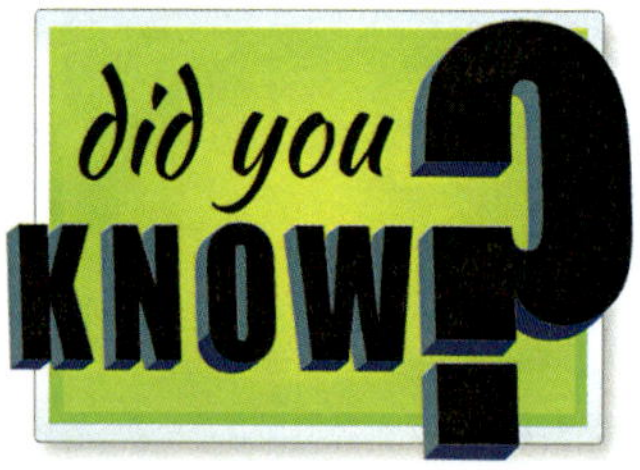

Unearned income, sometimes referred to as **passive income**, is income received although no work is performed, and no services are provided. Some examples of unearned income are retirement benefits, social security, disability payments, dividends and interest from investments, and child support. Another example of unearned income is money received from persons who rent or lease property from the property owner. If the owner does not actively participate in caring for the property and hires others to provide maintenance, the rent payment received after all expenses are paid is considered unearned, or passive, income.

EXERCISE 1.1

Complete the following exercise by indicating if the example on the left is either earned income (E), unearned income (U), or income that is not taxable (N). The first one is completed for you as an example.

Money received from working at a fast-food restaurant. __E___

1. Wages received for helping a neighbor clean their house. ________
2. Receiving a video game for mowing and raking the lawn of a friend. ________
3. Interest earned by a bank for money in a savings account. ________
4. Birthday money received from a parent living in the same house. ________
5. Child support money received. ________
6. Cash received from a person in your neighborhood for walking their dogs. ________
7. Cash received for babysitting younger siblings. ________
8. A gift card received for helping a person move. ________
9. Grant money received to go to college. ________
10. A bag of oranges received for a bag of avocados. ________

EXERCISE 1.2

Match terms with their definitions.

______ 1. Earned Income

______ 2. In-Kind

______ 3. Net Income

______ 4. IRS

______ 5. Revenue

______ 6. Unearned Income

a. Cash generated from the sales of goods and services by companies.

b. Money received for performing work or providing services.

c. Money received when work isn't performed or services are not provided. It is sometimes called passive income.

d. An item received in exchange for work performed or services provided.

e. The governmental agency that receives revenue through the collection of taxes.

f. The money that remains after expenses are subtracted from revenues.

LESSON 2 - EXPENSES

Expenses are costs spent on goods and services. Expenses are either fixed, variable, or discretionary. **Fixed expenses** are costs that do not change from month-to-month. These are costs that must be paid even if a person does not have the money to pay for them or if their income suddenly decreases. Several examples of fixed expenses are payments for rent or mortgage, an auto loan, and auto insurance bills. A mortgage could be refinanced for a lower monthly payment, a person could move to place with a lower rent payment, and the terms for auto insurance could be changed, but changes to these items are not made easily.

Variable expenses are the costs for necessary items that vary according to usage. In other words, variable expenses increase and decrease according to a person's activity. For example, utilities such as water, trash, and electricity are necessary expenses. Using water as an example of a utility and you as the customer, there is typically a minimum fixed cost associated with an account to access water from the water company such as $15 per month. The $15 is charged to you, the customer, every month regardless of how much water you use. The set, monthly access fee of $15 is a fixed expense. When you use the water, you are charged a per gallon fee. If the per gallon usage fee is $.25 per gallon and you used 100 gallons in a month, your monthly usage cost would be $25 and your total bill would be $40 which is the $15 monthly access fee added to the $40 usage fee. Your usage of the water may vary month-to-month. The variation in water usage from month-to-month is a variable expense.

Wants and needs are not the same!

Another example of variable costs is the use of a cell phone. Cell phone bills have a montly access fee that remains the same regardless of your usage of the cell phone. However, the monthly bill can increase according to usage outside of the stated plan terms. If you use more data than your plan allows, you may be charged additional fees, varying the amount you owe each month.

What about costs for eating out, going to the movie theater, or other types of entertainment? These costs are called **discretionary expenses**. Discretionary expenses are for things a person does not need to live. Engaging in activities such as renting a snow mobile for a day or going to a concert are fun, but not necessary to live.

Some expenses are tricky. For example, clothes and groceries are needed to live and vary according to preference and can be discretionary. For example, food and clothing are necessary to live, but the cost of these items can be reduced by buying non-brand-named products or items that are on sale. Additionally, snacks such as cookies, ice cream, and candy bars are discretionary purchases. Buying more pairs of shoes than needed are also discretionary purchases. Can you think of other examples of discretionary expenses?

EXERCISE 2

This crossword puzzle incorporates terms* learned in both lesson 1 and lesson 2. Using the definitions below the puzzle, enter the correct terms into the puzzle.

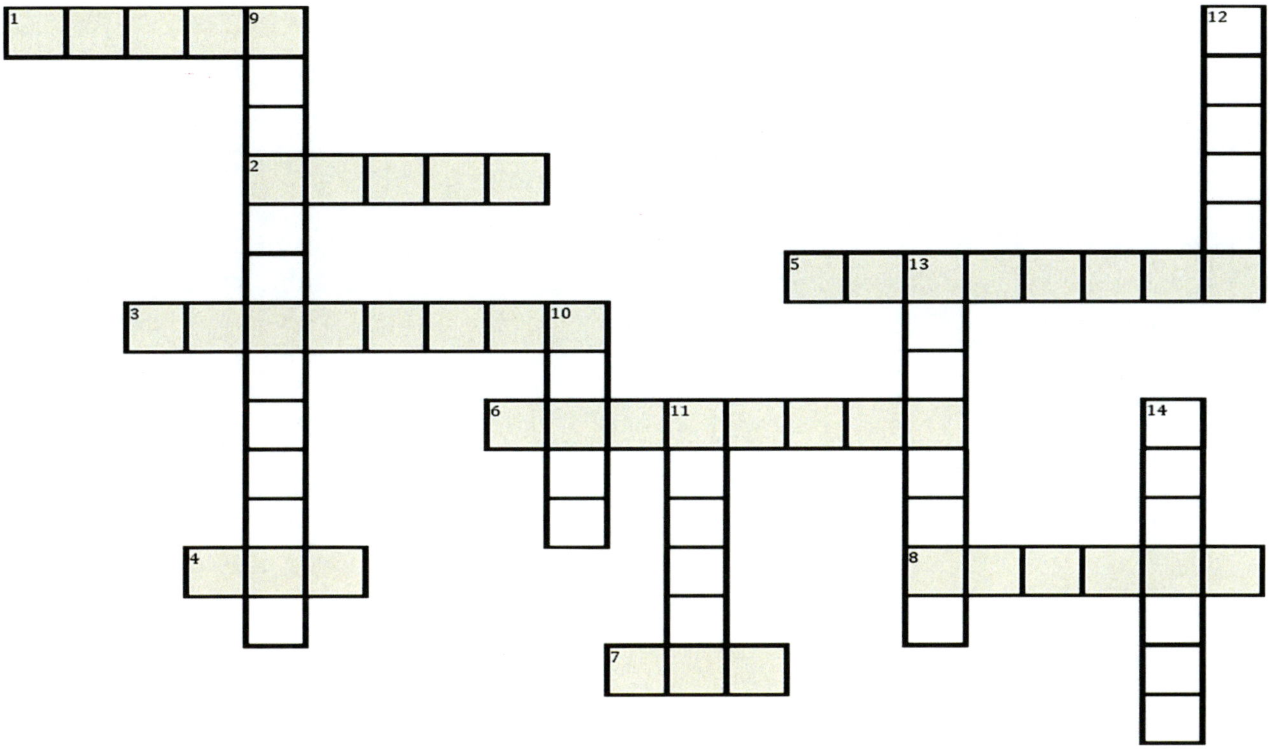

Across

1. An expense that is the same cost each month and must be paid.
2. Another word for expenses and identifies the price of an item.
3. An expense that doesn't have to be incurred. It's another word for discretionary.
4. The governmental agency that receives revenue through the collection of taxes.
5. Money received when work isn't performed or services are not provided. It is sometimes called passive income.
6. An expense that is still necessary, but can change from month to month.
7. The money that remains after expenses are subtracted from revenues.
8. Money received for performing work or providing services.

Down

9. Expenses that are optional, such as eating out.
10. What a financial institutional calls the money a customer borrows.
11. Wages and money earned from working.
12. An item received in exchange for work performed or services provided.
13. The cost or money spent on a something.
14. Cash generated from the sales of goods and services by companies.

**When the answer is "net income," only the word "net" is used in the puzzle.*

LESSON 3 - SAVINGS

Savings refers to money put aside for use at some point in the future. Saving money is beneficial for many reasons. It opens up purchase and/or investment opportunities in the future, meets financial goals, allows for payment of expenses when income is decreased or stopped for a period of time, earns money while not being used, and provides a source of income for retirement.

The most common way to save money is with a savings account at a financial institution such as a credit union, bank, or savings and loan. Savings accounts are also called deposit accounts. It is important to note that credit unions refer to savings accounts as **share accounts**. At credit unions, the depositior must qualify for membership. Different credit unions have different membership qualifications. Membership means each account holder at a particular credit union owns a **share** in the credit union. Members are also considered **shareholders** of that credit union because they own shares in the credit union. Every financial institution has a variety of savings products, which typically includes regular savings accounts, money market deposit accounts, certificates of deposits (CDs), automatic or club savings accounts, and IRA savings accounts. Each type of savings account requires a minimum balance and pays varying interest rates. Banks call the rate used to earn money in deposit accounts **interest rates;** whereas, credit unions call the rate for deposit accounts a **dividend rate**. A **dividend** is the money paid by a company to their shareholders.

Make sure to save each time you get paid!

Regular savings accounts usually have the smallest required minimum balance and pay the smallest interest. Money market deposit accounts require a larger minimum balance and pay more interest. As long as the minimum balance is maintained in these two types of savings accounts, a person can withdraw and deposit freely. However, it is important to note that Federal law requires financial institutions to charge a fee once a savings account exceeds six (6) withdrawals in a given month.

CDs function differently than regular savings and money market deposit accounts. With CDs, money is deposited once and held in the CD savings account for the agreed upon term. The deposited money must remain in the account until it matures in order to receive all of the earned interest. The **maturity date** is the date at the end of the term. If any or all of the money in the CD is withdrawn early, all of the earned interest is forfeited. CD terms range from 3 to 60 months, or

Minimum Balance	$ 1,000	$ 10,000	$ 20,000	$ 50,000	$ 100,000
Short-Term Certificate Rates					
3 Month	0.30%	0.30%	0.35%	0.35%	0.40%
6 Month	0.40%	0.40%	0.45%	0.45%	0.50%
9 Month	0.50%	0.50%	0.55%	0.55%	0.60%
12 Month	0.60%	0.60%	0.65%	0.65%	0.70%
18 Month	0.70%	0.70%	0.75%	0.75%	0.80%
24 Month	0.80%	0.80%	0.85%	0.85%	0.90%
Long-Term Certificate Rates					
3 Year	1.05%	1.05%	1.10%	1.10%	1.15%
4 year	1.15%	1.15%	1.20%	1.20%	1.25%
5 year	1.25%	1.25%	1.30%	1.30%	1.35%

longer. Interest rates tend to be higher for CD accounts. The interest rate varies according to how much a person deposits for a set term and is set by the financial institution. The illustration below shows what a CD product chart looks like:

As you can see from the illustration, if a person deposits $1,000 into a 3-Month CD, the interest rate would be .30%; whereas, if they deposit $1,000 into a 3-Year CD, the interest rate would be 1.05%. Depositing a larger sum of money for a longer period of time earns more money.

Another type of savings account that pays higher interest rates at some institutions is club accounts, which are basically automatic savings accounts. These accounts either withdraw a predetermined amount of money from a checking account or an automatic paycheck deposit. The account holder sets the amount withdrawn; however, there is sometimes a minimum and/or maximum monthly deposit amount required. These accounts also require the account holder to leave all deposited funds in the account for the agreed upon term, which is normally a year. A variety of club accounts exist to meet consumer needs or demands: Christmas/Holiday, Vacation, and Wedding to name a few.

The last savings account type discussed in this Chapter is an IRA account. This discussion will be brief as more information is shared in the Investments Section. An IRA savings account requires a one-time, lump sum or regular monthly deposit that will be used for retirement. Once money is deposited into an IRA account, it cannot be withdrawn early without losing the interest earned and paying an **early withdrawal penalty**.

Why do financial institutions pay people for their deposits? Why do the rates vary among institutions? In simple terms, financial institutions use the money deposited into savings accounts in their institution to fund the loans they give to people for houses, autos, credit cards, etc. Financial institutions go through cycles of needing more or less deposit funds. They use interest rates to attract or dissuade people from depositing money. They offer higher interest rates when they need more deposits and lower interest rates when they need fewer deposits.

An astute investor will use a variety of savings accounts. Sometimes money is needed quickly. When that is the case, it is good to have money in a savings product that is liquid, or from which it is easy to withdraw funds. Because money in a regular savings account does not earn much, it is also a good idea to have money in another savings account that earns a higher interest rate but requires a longer commitment. One way to have multiple CDs without having maturity dates at the same time is to ladder CD accounts. **Laddering** means opening several CDs with staggered maturity dates. For example, Donna has $8,000 to invest in CDs, but does not want to tie up all of the money for an extended period of time, she could open four CDs for $2,000 each, for example a 6-month, a 12-month, an 18-month, and a 24-month CD. Because CDs are not considered liquid, the investor must be okay with waiting the agreed upon time for each CD to mature. In this example, if the 6-month CD matures and the money is not needed, the CD can be allowed to automatically renew for another 6-months. This would keep the CD maturity dates laddered and the money available in a reasonable time frame.

Early withdrawals may have penalties!

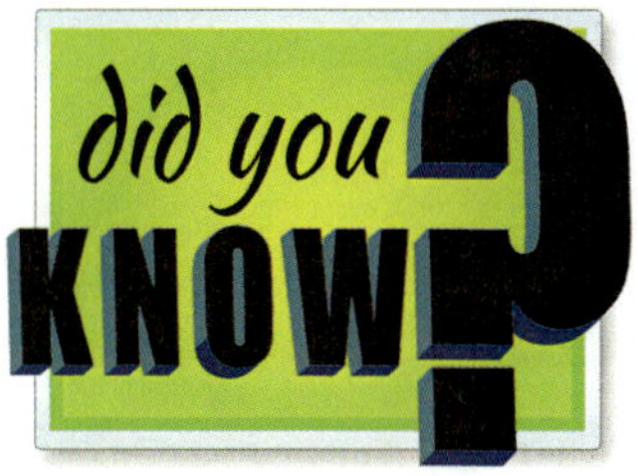

Knowing how much money, or interest, will be earned in a given account over a particular amount

of time can be easily calculated in three ways: use the "future value" formula by hand, use a financial calculator using the formula, or use an online annuity calculator. In the following example, Billy wants to know how much interest he will earn in a year if he opens a Vacation Club savings account paying 2% interest at ABC Financial Institution. He chooses to deposit $500 when opening the account and will deposit an additional $100 each month. Using an online financial calculator for simple savings, Billy determines he will have $1,721.15 at the end of the first year. The total amount of money he deposits during the year, including his initial investment, is $1,600. The interest he would earn is $121.15. Billy plans to let his money work for him. Of course, the more he deposits, the more interest he will earn.

Laddering CDs

diversifies

interest rate risk!

Different philosophies exist about saving money. Investing a reasonable amount and being consistent is a good way to start. As the opportunity presents itself, the investor should diversify their savings as discussed earlier. **Diversifying** means to use a variety of savings options with some being liquid with lower interest and some harder to cash in but with higher interest rates. Having diversified savings prepares the investor for situations such as a job loss or a surprise expense.

EXERCISE 3.1

Fill in the blanks:

1. Putting money aside for future events is called ______________________________.

2. Name three benefits to having a savings account: ______________________________, ______________________________, and, ______________________________.

3. A ______________________________ is used to save money at a financial institution.

4. Credit unions refer to savings accounts as __________________________ accounts.

5. Members at credit unions are known as ______________________________.

6. Most financial institutions pay __________________________ for deposits into savings accounts using an ______________________________ ______________________________ to determine how much they will pay.

7. Money paid to a shareholder of a company is called ______________________________.

8. A person would pay a penalty called ______________________ ______________________ ______________________ for withdrawing money before the specified time on an IRA.

9. Financial institutions need deposits in order to fund ____________________ to consumers.

10. Quick access to money means it is __________________________.

11. In order to have multiple CDs maturity dates, a person would ____________________ the CDs.

12. Determining the upcoming worth of an investment is called the ______________________ ______________________?

13. Determining the future value of an investment can be done by using an online ______________________.

14. Savings should be ______________________________ in order to be prepare for all circumstances.

EXERCISE 3.2

Using the following CD product chart, answer the questions.

Minimum Balance	$ 1,000	$ 10,000	$ 20,000	$ 50,000	$ 100,000
Short-Term Certificate Rates					
3 Month	0.10%	0.15%	0.20%	0.25%	0.30%
6 Month	0.35%	0.40%	0.45%	0.50%	0.55%
9 Month	0.60%	0.65%	0.70%	0.75%	0.80%
12 Month	0.85%	0.90%	0.95%	0.10%	1.05%
18 Month	1.10%	1.15%	1.20%	1.25%	1.30%
24 Month	1.35%	1.40%	1.45%	1.50%	1.55%
Long-Term Certificate Rates					
3 Year	1.60%	1.65%	1.70%	1.75%	1.80%
4 year	1.85%	1.90%	1.95%	2.00%	2.05%
5 year	2.10%	2.15%	2.20%	2.25%	2.30%

1. The interest rate for a 3-month CD with a $10,000 deposit would be ______________ %.

2. What CD term would a person need to select to get a rate of 2.20%?

   ___________________________.

3. How much money would a person need to get a rate of 2.05% for a 4 Year term?

   ___________________________.

4. Susie chooses a 3-year CD that has an interest rate of 1.75%. Upon maturity of the CD, she has a balance of $52,671.21. How much was her initial deposit? ____________________. How much interest did she make? _______________________.

LESSON 4 - GIVING

Giving is freely contributing something to someone else without the expectation of receiving anything in return. This can be done by donating money to a non-profit organization such as a church or the United Way, giving something of material value to a person in need or to a charitable organization such as a thrift store, or providing time to help others.

The decision to give is an individual one which cannot be determined by looking at what others give because incomes, expenses, and available personal time vary. How much should a person give? According to the Nonprofits Source website, 17% of Americans tithe a portion of their income. Opinions vary about if, when, and how much individuals should tithe. Sometimes giving money is not possible for an individual due to very low income or no job, but during those times, a person may still be able to give their time. If one were to go to five different people and ask the best method or how much to give, they would probably get five different answers. Regardless of how much a person gives, giving has positive emotional benefits. There is a sense of accomplishment when helping where there is a need.

This lesson, however, focuses on the financial aspect of giving. Donating money or material items of value provides a tax benefit for those who are able to claim deductions, but this is not usually the case for those who have not purchased a house or had children. However, understanding the benefit of deductions for charitable donations is part of a better understanding of personal finance.

Claiming personal deductions on a tax return means itemizing those deductions. **Itemizing** deductions is listing all allowable deductions in order to lower your taxable income. Lowering taxable income results in lowering **tax liability** or how much is owed in taxes. Personal deductions, such as donations to non-profit organizations, can reduce an individual's tax liability.

Each year, when completing tax forms, taxpayers choose either a 1040EZ, 1040A, or a 1040. Basically, the 1040EZ is for those who are not itemizing their deductions. The 1040A is used when an individual is claiming certain tax credits but not itemizing deductions. The 1040 is for those who are itemizing their deductions and claiming tax credits. Once you are no longer a dependent of your parents or another adult, you can claim the standard deduction that is allowed each year. In simple terms, a standard deduction is the amount of money that can be deducted from the taxes you owe. As an example of the standard deduction amount, the standard deduction for a single taxpayer was $6,300 in 2015.

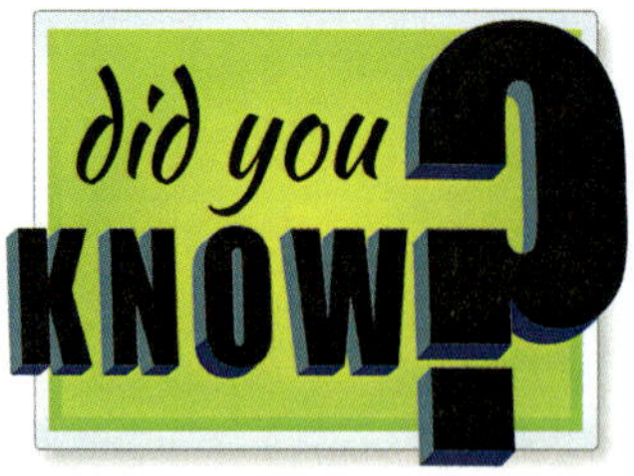

Giving should be done without expecting anything in return.

Many people do not know when to itemize their deductions. Itemizing deductions should begin when an individual's or couple's deductions total more than the standard allowed deduction. Itemized deductions include home mortgage expenses, charitable donations, property taxes, state income taxes, medical expenses, etc. For charitable donations, it not only includes money given but items of value, such as clothing and toys, donated to a non-profit organization.

EXAMPLE 4-1

Suppose: Susie is a freshman in college and has a job making $10,000 a year. In February, she sits down to do her taxes. Last year she gave $500 to a non-profit organization and some old clothes, worth $100, to a local charity. She does not have any other deductions. Her parents are claiming her as a dependent on their taxes. Which tax form would Susie mostly likely use?

Answer: Susie would use the 1040EZ form. Since her parents claim her as a dependent, Susie cannot claim the single taxpayer deduction. Additionally, if Susie could claim herself, her $600 in charitable deduction does not exceed the single taxpayer deduction.

EXAMPLE 4-2

Suppose: Susie lives on her own, claims herself as a dependent, purchased a house, and makes $40,000 a year. In March, she sits down to do her taxes. Last year she gave $4,000 to a non-profit organization and some personal items, worth $700, to a local charity. She volunteered 100 hours at a non-profit animal shelter, which she thinks is worth $10 an hour, or $1,000. She paid $1,500 on home mortgage insurance and $1,100 in property taxes. She does not have any other deductions. How much are her deductions? Which tax form would she use if she itemizes her deductions?

Answer: Susie's deductions total $7,300 ($4,000+$700+$1,500+$1,100). Susie cannot claim time that is volunteered to a non-profit, only money and items of value. She would use Form 1040 because she is itemizing her deductions.

Money donated to a non-profit organization for the purposes of a tax deduction is only deductible if given without receiving anything in return. For example, if a person gives $25 to the Girls Scouts as a donation and does not receive anything in return, $25 can be used as a tax deduction.

However, if a person gives $25 to the Girl's Scouts and receives cookies in exchange, that $25 is not tax deductible.

Giving money to non-profits, such as churches or charitable organizations, is an important aspect of life, and the IRS has sought to allow an economic benefit for those who do. It is important to remember there is more than an economic benefit to giving.

EXERCISE 4

True or False and Multiple Choice Problems:

1. True or False. Itemizing deductions is listing all non-allowable deductions in order to lower one's taxable income.

2. Which of the following describes giving:

    a. Giving money to a person out of force.
    b. Paying a bill that is due.
    c. Walking a neighbor's dog in exchange for a bag of oranges.
    d. Freely giving something to someone without expecting anything in return.
    e. All of these.

3. True or False. A tax liability is the amount of tax a person or company owes.

4. The simple tax form used when a person isn't itemizing their deductions is called:

    a. 1040
    b. 1004EZ
    c. 1040EZ
    d. 1040A

5. True or False. When itemizing deductions for taxes, a person would use the 1040 tax form.

6. True or False. A person can use volunteer hours at a charitable organization as tax deduction.

7. True or False. There are many different attitudes towards how much to give.

8. A person has the following itemized deductions: \$500 for mortgage interest; \$900 for property taxes; \$3,000 donations to a church; and \$50 for buying popcorn from the Boy Scouts. How much is their allowable tax deductions:

    a. \$4,400
    b. \$4,450
    c. \$4,475
    d. \$3,900

9. True or False. There are positive emotional benefits to the giver when they give to others.

10. True or False. Volunteering one's time to help others is a form of giving.

QUIZ - SECTION 1

True or False:

1. True or False. The term 'revenue' is typically used to describe personal income.
2. True or False. Variable expenses are those that are the same each month.
3. True or False. Savings is putting money aside to use the future.
4. True or False. Itemizing deductions for tax purposes is listing all allowable deductions.
5. True or False. The IRS is a charitable organization for homeless people.
6. True or False. Discretionary expenses are not the same as variable expenses.
7. True or False. Dividends are paid by a company to their employees as wages.
8. True or False. Giving is being forced to give something to someone without an expectation of anything in return.
9. True or False. An in-kind payment is when a person receives something of value in exchange for work performed.
10. True or False. The maturity date on a loan is when the loan begins.

Multiple Choice Problems:

11. Which of the following is NOT an example of earned income:

    a. Wages received from working at the local fast-food restaurant.
    b. Interest earned from money in a CD.
    c. Cash received for raking a neighbor's lawn.
    d. Money received for helping a friend move.

12. Which of the following is the definition of fixed expenses;

    a. Costs that change from month-to-month.
    b. Buying an expense cost.
    c. Costs that do not change from month-to-month.
    d. a and b above
    e. None of the above.

13. What is an early withdrawal penalty:

    a. Money due for stopping piano lessons.
    b. Money due for withdrawing money from a regular savings account.
    c. Money due for not paying taxes on time.
    d. Money due for withdrawing money out of an IRA before the specified time.

14. Which of the following in NOT an example of giving:

    a. Buying a book from a non-profit organization.
    b. Giving money to a local church.
    c. Volunteering time at a local library.
    d. Paying for a meal for a friend who is hungry.

15. What is another word for unearned income:

    a. Produced
    b. Created
    c. Passive
    d. Generated

16. What is another name for a savings account at a credit union:

    a. Gift account
    b. Share account
    c. Club account
    d. Reserves account

17. Which of the following is an example of a discretionary expenses:

    a. Utility bills
    b. Eating at a fancy restaurant
    c. Rent payment
    d. Groceries

18. If a person wants to claim their charitable donations on their taxes, which form would they use:

    a. 1014EZ
    b. 1040EZ
    c. 1014
    d. 1040

19. A person received a baseball mitt in exchange for cleaning a neighbor's pool. What type of income would this be:

    a. Earned income
    b. In-kind income
    c. Unearned income
    d. Passive income

20. Expenses that vary in cost, but are needed each month are called:

    a. Fixed expenses
    b. Variety expenses
    c. Variable expenses
    d. Future expenses

21. Which of the following describes a savings account that is liquid:

    a. A regular savings account where money can be withdrawn in a day.
    b. A CD where money can be withdrawn in a day, but all interest is lost.
    c. An IRA account for retirement.
    d. A club account where money can be withdrawn in a day, but all interest is lost.

22. What does IRS represent:

    a. Internal Routing Service
    b. Installment Revenue Service
    c. Income Revenue Service
    d. Internal Revenue Service

23. What does it mean to diversify with savings:

    a. To use a variety of products for savings.
    b. To only use one savings account.
    c. To open five CD accounts.
    d. To open more than one checking account.

24. Which of the following represents laddering CD accounts:

    a. Opening four 6-month CDs on the day.
    b. Opening a 24-month CD.
    c. Opening a 6-month, 12-month, 18-month, and 24-month CD on the same day.
    d. None of these represent laddering CD accounts.

25. Which is the best benefit of giving:

    a. Knowing others in need have been helped.
    b. Possibly lowering one's tax liability.
    c. Feeling a sense of gratitude.
    d. All of these are benefits of giving.

SECTION 2 - ASSETS

KEYWORDS

Accounts receivable

Appraisal

Asset

Commodities

Current assets

Fixed assets

Intangible assets

Liabilities

Long-term assets

Marketable securities

Notes receivable

Personal financial statements

Personal net worth

Personal property

Prepaid asset

Short-term asset

Tangible assets

LEARNING OBJECTIVES FOR SECTION 2

Upon successful completion of Section 2, you will be able to:

- Classify assets into short or long-term.
- Complete the asset section on a personal financial statement.

LESSON 5 - ASSETS ~ WHAT IS OWNED

In general, an asset is something of value. It includes talents, friends, and material possessions. Think about something or someone who is of value to you. Assets, in general, are different for each person.

More specifically, in the world of personal finance, an asset is an item of value that is owned by an individual. This type of asset can come in various forms: fixed, tangible, short-term, and long-term.

Personal net worth should be positive!

Assets are part of your **personal net worth**. Understanding what is owned (assets) is one part of the equation determining a person's net worth and thereby understanding their financial health. To determine your personal net worth, subtract your total **liabilities** (debts that you owe) from your total assets. (Liabilities are discussed in further detail in Section 3.) Why is this calculation important? Because if your net worth is negative, you have too many debt obligations. In other words, you do not have enough assets to sell off in order to pay all of your liabilities.

To get started, let's discuss fixed assets and personal property. **Fixed assets** are tangible items that are usually owned for a long time and are not expected to be sold or converted to cash. Examples of fixed assets are houses, property, vehicles, large equipment, and personal property. Personal property consists of assets that can be moved from one place to another. This category includes assets such as jewelry, computers, furniture, stocks, bonds, clothing, antiques, retirement funds, CDs, books, video games, and musical instruments.

Some fixed assets, such as houses and property, may increase in value over time while others, such as vehicles and computers, decrease in value over time. The value of some fixed assets can fluctuate, such as assets tied to the price of commodities. **Commodities** are basic goods, such as raw materials, that are used in the manufacturing of products. Most commodities fluctuate in value because they are tied to the commodities market. For example, the value of jewelry made of gold or silver will increase or decrease with the price of gold or silver in the commodities market.

It is important to determine an accurate value for each asset owned. Appraisals determine the value of items and can be used to determine the value of things such as a house, jewelry, antiques, paintings, and power tools. An **appraisal** consists of an expert giving an estimated value of specific a property or product. A car's value can be determined by using online websites such as the National Automobile Dealers Association (NADA) website. Determining the value of personal property is tricky as most personal property depreciates (decreases) over time. While some personal property items can be appraised, it is difficult to give a value to everyday items such as clothing. After determining the value of items through an appraisal, the remaining cash value of all personal property for one person is roughly $5,000 or $10,000 for a two-adult household.

EXERCISE 5.1

List the assets you own:

________________________ ________________________

________________________ ________________________

________________________ ________________________

________________________ ________________________

________________________ ________________________

________________________ ________________________

________________________ ________________________

________________________ ________________________

EXERCISE 5.2

Match words with their definitions.

1. Asset
2. Fixed asset
3. Personal property
4. Liability
5. Appraisal
6. NADA
7. Personal net worth

a. National Automobile Dealers Association

b. An estimated value of property or a good by a expert.

c. Something of value.

d. An item that can be moved from one place to another place.

e. That which indicates a person's financial health.

f. A tangible item typically held for longer than one year.

g. That which is owed.

LESSON 6 - SHORT-TERM ASSETS

A **short-term asset** is an asset that will be sold, or converted to cash, within a year. Examples of short-term assets are cash, marketable securities, and prepaid rent or insurance. **Marketable securities** are assets such as common stock and government bonds that can be easily converted to cash within a year. Short-term assets are also known as **current assets**.

Short-term and current assets are the same.

A **prepaid asset** exists when something is paid for before it becomes due. For example, paying your auto insurance for the next six months or year in order to receive a decrease in the insurance rate is a prepaid asset. The prepaid insurance then becomes a short-term asset. The value of the asset decreases each month it is used. If you, the policy holder, cancels the policy three months into the policy term, you will receive a refund for entire term and minus the time the policy was in effect.

EXAMPLE 6-1

Suppose: On January 1, Jennifer pays $1,200 for a 12-month auto insurance policy that goes from January 1 to December 31. If Jennifer cancels the policy on June 30, or six months into her policy plan, how much would she get back from the insurance company?

Answer: $600. Jennifer's prepaid insurance is valued at $1,200 for 12 months, or $100 per month ($1,200 / 12 = $100). If Jennifer cancels her policy effective June 30, she would have six remaining months that were prepaid.

An asset that is not originally a short-term asset can become a short-term asset as time passes. For example, a 3-year CD is not a short-term asset when initially started; however, once the maturity date of the 3-year CD is within a year, it becomes a short-term asset.

EXAMPLE 6-2

Suppose: On January 1, 2019, Sally invested $10,000 in a 3-year CD with a maturity date of December 31, 2022. When does Sally's CD investment become a short-term asset?

Answer: Sally's CD investment will become a short-term asset as of January 1, 2022, because the maturity date of December 31, 2022, is within 3 years of January 1, 2022.

EXERCISE 6

True or False and Multiple Choice Problems:

1. True or False. A short-term asset is an asset that can be sold, or convert to cash, within 24 months.

2. A short-term asset is also known as:

    a. Existing asset
    b. Prepaid asset
    c. Current asset
    d. Present asset

3. True or False. A prepaid asset is when a bill is paid before it becomes due.

Using the following scenario, answer questions 4 through 6.

George makes a deal with his landlord to pay for all of his rent for the next year for a reduce monthly rate. His landlord agrees to accept $500 per month. George pays for 12 months of rent on June 1, 2013, with $500 going towards June's rent.

4. What type of asset does George have with paying his rent ahead:

    a. Prepaid asset
    b. Long-term asset
    c. Fixed asset
    d. Appraised asset

5. How much rent did George pay to his landlord:

    a. $500
    b. $3,000
    c. $6,000
    d. $8,000

6. On December 31, 2013, what is the value of George's prepaid asset:

    a. $6,000
    b. $500
    c. $3,000
    d. $2,500

7. Rick started a 2-year CD on July 1, 2013. What does the CD become a short-term asset:

    a. December 31, 2013
    b. July 1, 2014
    c. April 1, 2014
    d. July 1, 2013

LESSON 7 - LONG-TERM ASSETS

Long-term assets, also known as fixed assets, were discussed briefly in Lesson 5. Long-term assets are also known as noncurrent assets. In business, long-term, tangible assets are classified as property, plant, and equipment (PP&E). However, some long-term assets are intangible assets.

Tangible assets have a physical state and can be seen or touched. An **intangible** asset is something that cannot be seen or touched because it does not have a physical state. Examples of intangible assets are patents, copyrights, brand names, intellectual property, and reputation.

Intangible assets cannot be seen or touched!

Long-term assets are permanent in nature and will not be turned into cash within a year. For example, people generally purchase long-term investments such as houses, land, and cars with the intend to hold the assets for longer than a year. However, the unexpected happens and while a person may have a long-term asset they did not plan to sell within the next year, they may suddenly need to sell earlier than expected.

Another type of long-term asset is **accounts and notes receivable**. If you loan money to another person or company, and the loan will be paid back to you in full within a year, it falls into the category of short-term notes receivable. Conversely, if it will take longer than a year for the loan to be fully repaid, the asset is in the long-term accounts receivable category.

EXAMPLE 7-1

Suppose: Henry and Susan own a farm. What could be some of their short and long-term assets be?

Answer: Short-term assets may include cash, harvested crops, feed for animals, prepaid expenses, and cattle to be sold within the next year. Long-term assets may include buildings, land, machinery, breeding stock, and cattle held for more than a year.

EXAMPLE 7-2

Suppose: Mike and Rebecca own a house, have a checking and savings account, have auto insurance which they paid for the entire year, and sold a car to a friend, Bill, who is paying monthly payments to them. The personal car loan to Bill will be paid in full in 24 months. What could be some of the Mike and Rebecca's short and long-term assets?

Answer: Short-term assets may include cash, clothing, and prepaid expenses. Their long-term assets could include the house, jewelry, lawn equipment, cars, paintings, furniture, and the car loan to Bill.

EXERCISE 7

True or False and Multiple Choice Problems:

1. True or False. Long-term assets are also known as fixed, tangible, and noncurrent assets.

2. Which of the following are examples of tangible assets for a business:
    a. Property, plant, and equipment
    b. Trademark
    c. Reputation
    d. Copyright

3. Which of the following is an example of a personal tangible asset:
    a. List of friends
    b. Number of friends on Facebook
    c. Patent
    d. Land

4. Which of the following is an example of an intangible asset:
    a. 2014 Chevy Truck
    b. Motorcycle
    c. Copyright for a book
    d. House

5. True or False. A person can suddenly decide to sell a long-term asset.

6. Which of the following is the definition of a long-term asset:
    a. An item that will likely be sold, or converted to cash, within a year.
    b. An item permanent in nature that will not be turned to cash within a year.
    c. An item that can be used for a really long time.
    d. A 6-month CD.

7. True or False. Short and long-term assets mean the same thing?

8. Which of the following would be a long-term asset on a farm:
    a. Cattle held for more than one year
    b. Machinery
    c. Buildings and land
    d. All of these answers are long-term assets on a farm

9. Which of the following would be a short-term asset of a homeowner:
    a. House
    b. Marketable securities
    c. Lawnmower
    d. Retirement account

10. True or False. Rent pre-paid for three years is a long-term asset?

LESSON 8 - ASSET SECTION ON A PERSONAL FINANCIAL STATEMENT

Personal Financial Statements (PFS) come in several formats with some being more detailed than others. The first, or top, section contains personal information such as name, address, contact information, and social security number. The second section is for listing all assets. Some PFSs separate current assets from noncurrent assets and then total them for total assets. The third section is for listing all liabilities. There may also be a section to list income and contingent liabilities (to be explained in Section 3). Many PFSs have a second page that explains assets and liabilities by listing them separately. Totals are shown on the first page.

The following illustration is an example of the asset section on a personal financial statement.

ASSETS	DOLLARS Round to the nearest whole dollar
Cash on Hand at Financial institutions	$ ______
Savings Accounts	$ ______
IRA or Other Retirement Accounts	$ ______
Accounts & Notes Receivable	$ ______
Life Insurance - Cash Surrender Value Only ..	$ ______
Stocks and Bonds	$ ______
Real Estate	$ ______
Automobile Present Value	$ ______
Other - Personal Property	$ ______
Other Assets	$ ______
Total	$ ______

Each line is explained as follows:

Cash on Hand at Financial Institutions – any money a person has in cash or in their checking accounts.

Savings Accounts – any money in any type of savings account, which would include CDs.

IRA or Other Retirement Accounts – money in an IRA or any other type of retirement account such as a 401K.

Accounts & Notes Receivable – money that has been loaned to a person or company and is expected to be paid back.

Life Insurance – Cash Surrender Value Only – Some life insurance policies have a cash value that has been built into the policy.

Stocks and Bonds – the value of stocks and bonds owned by a person.

Real Estate – the value of buildings and land.

Automobile Present Value – value of all owned vehicles (autos, motorcycles, trucks, etc.), this includes those with loans.

Other – Personal Property – value of all personal property such as jewelry, clothing, antiques, appliances, etc.

Other Assets – value of goods not listed such as recreational vehicles and boats.

EXERCISE 8

Using the following information, fill in the list of assets below and total them.

Thomas has the following assets.

- $5,000 IRA account
- A boat worth $7,000
- $250 in a box at home
- A truck with a $10,000 value
- Personal property of $5,000
- A motorcycle with a value of $3,000
- $4,000 in his checking account
- A 401K account with a $25,000 balance
- His sister owes him $1,500 for a car
- His house is worth $95,000
- He has a $1,000 CD and $5,000 in a money market savings account
- He doesn't own any stocks or bonds.
- His life insurance policy has a cash surrender value of $2,000
- He has land worth $10,000
- He owns antiques valued at $23,000

ASSETS	DOLLARS Round to the nearest whole dollar
Cash on Hand at Financial institutions	$ ______________
Savings Accounts	$ ______________
IRA or Other Retirement Accounts	$ ______________
Accounts & Notes Receivable	$ ______________
Life Insurance - Cash Surrender Value Only ..	$ ______________
Stocks and Bonds	$ ______________
Real Estate	$ ______________
Automobile Present Value	$ ______________
Other - Personal Property	$ ______________
Other Assets	$ ______________
Total	$ ______________

QUIZ - SECTION 2

True or False:

1. True or False. Accounts receivable is a noncurrent asset.
2. True or False. Notes receivable is a current asset.
3. True or False. A trademark is an intangible asset.
4. True or False. Land is considered a long-term asset.
5. True or False. Another term for long-term asset is long-standing asset.
6. True or False. Paying for February's rent on February 1st is considered a prepaid asset.
7. True or False. NADA is one of many companies that offer values for vehicles.
8. True or False. A short-term asset is sold or converted to cash within a year.
9. True or False. A long-term asset is permanent in nature.
10. True or False. PFS stands for Professional Finance Status.

Using the following scenario, answer questions 11 through 14.

On December 31, 2012, Caleb obtained a discount for his auto insurance and paid upfront for an entire year of coverage that begins January 1, 2013, and ends December 31, 2013. His insurance cost is $200 per month.

11. What type of asset does Caleb have with paying a year of auto insurance before it is due:
    a. Prepaid asset
    b. Long-term asset
    c. Fixed asset
    d. Appraised asset

12. How much did Caleb pay to his insurance agent:
    a. $200
    b. $1,200
    c. $2,400
    d. $1,800

13. On June 30, 2013, what is the value of Caleb's prepaid asset:
    a. $2,400
    b. $1,200
    c. $200
    d. $1,400

14. If Caleb were to cancel his insurance effective April 1, 2013, how much money would the insurance company return to him for unused insurance premiums:

a. $1,200
b. $200
c. $0
d. $1,800

Using the following information, fill in the list of assets below and total them.

Caleb has the following assets.

- He has $30,000 in a 401K account
- $500 in a box at home
- Personal property of $5,000
- $6,000 in his checking account
- His friend owes him $2,500 for a loan
- He has two CDs with a balance of $3,000 each and $5,000 in a money market savings account
- He has a house worth $100,000
- He owns jewelry valued at $20,000
- He owns an RV worth $12,500
- A car with a $10,000 value
- Prepaid insurance valued at $2,400
- He has three IRA accounts with a balance of $2,500 in each one
- He has farm land worth $50,000
- He doesn't own any stocks or bonds.
- His life insurance policy has a cash surrender value of $2,000

ASSETS	DOLLARS Round to the nearest whole dollar
15. Cash on Hand at Financial institutions	$ ________
16. Savings Accounts	$ ________
17. IRA or Other Retirement Accounts	$ ________
18. Accounts & Notes Receivable	$ ________
19. Life Insurance - Cash Surrender Value Only ..	$ ________
20. Stocks and Bonds	$ ________
21. Real Estate	$ ________
22. Automobile Present Value	$ ________
23. Other - Personal Property	$ ________
24. Other Assets	$ ________
25. Total	$ ________

SECTION 3 - LIABILITIES

KEYWORDS

Contingent liabilities

Equity

Installments loans

Liability

Long-term liabilities

Outstanding balance

Overextended

Payday loans

Personal cash flow statement

Short-term liabilities

LEARNING OBJECTIVES FOR SECTION 3

Upon successful completion of Section 3, you will be able to:

- Differentiate between assets and liablilities.
- Complete the liability section on a personal financial statement.
- Classify liabilities into short-term, long-term, or contingent.

LESSON 9 - LIABILITIES ~ WHAT IS OWED

Anything a person is responsible for is a liability, in general terms. A liability can also be a hindrance such as a negative attitude or the lack of a skill. In finance and accounting, a **liability** is a debt or money that is owed. As was discussed earlier, an asset is what you own. Liabilities, like assets, are described as short and long-term.

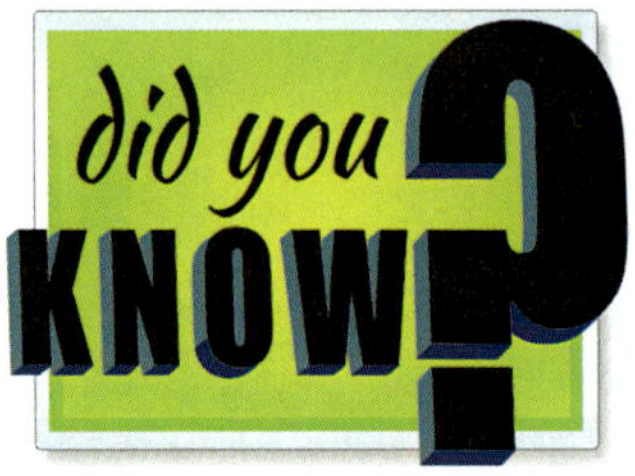

Financial liabilities are debts that are owed.

A person can have an item that is both an asset and a liability. For instance, if you had a house loan, the house would be an asset because it is owned; however, the loan for the house is a liability because it is owed. The equity in the house is the difference between how much is owed and the value of the house. In other words, **equity** is the value in a property after all debts attached to the property are subtracted.

EXAMPLE 9-1

Suppose: Rebecca has a house loan for $100,000 and her house has a value of $150,000. What are the values of her asset and her liability for the house? How much equity does she have in the house?

Answer: The house would be listed as an asset for $150,000 and the loan on the house would be listed as a liability for $100,000. The equity in the house would be $50,000.

One goal with finances is to keep total assets greater than total liabilities. There are several personal finance ratios to help determine the health of your financial situation. One such ratio is the debt ratio. To calculate a debt ratio, total debt is divided by total assets. A debt ratio of more than 100% means you have more debt than you have assets to sell for cash to pay off all of your debt. A debt ratio of 50% or less is good, but 30% or less is much better.

EXAMPLE 9-2

Suppose: Rebecca has an auto loan for $15,000 and a house loan for $100,000. Her assets total $160,000. What is her debt ratio? Is her debt ratio good or high?

Answer: Rebecca's debt ratio is 72% ($115,000 / $160,000 = 0.71875). This debt ratio is a bit high. Rebecca should try to lower her debt ratio to below 50%. The best way for her to do this is to pay down her loans.

EXERCISE 9

True or False and Multiple Choice Problems:

1. Which of the following would be a personal liability:
    a. Negative attitude
    b. Lacking a necessary skill
    c. Both a and b
    d. Neither a and b

2. True or False. A liability in finance or accounting is that which is owned.

3. Which of the following defines equity:
    a. The difference between a car loan and a house loan.
    b. The difference between the value of an item and what is owed on the same item.
    c. Debt owed.
    d. None of these defines equity.

4. If total debts equal $120,000 and total assets equal $250,000, what is the debt ratio:
    a. 40%
    b. 52%
    c. 2.08%
    d. 48%

5. What is the best debt ratio of the four possibilities below:
    a. 50%
    b. 75%
    c. 100%
    d. 125%

6. True or False. Having more total debt than total assets is good.

7. True or False. Total assets divided by total debt is the debt ratio formula.

8. How much equity does a person have in a property if it valued at $225,000 and they have a loan for $175,000:
    a. $225,000
    b. $50,000
    c. $175,000
    d. $75,000

9. True or False. The goal with finances is to have more total assets than total liabilities.

10. True or False. A debt ratio is only one of many ratios to determine the health of a person's finances.

LESSON 10 - SHORT-TERM LIABILITIES

Short-term liabilities are also known as current liabilities. These are debts or obligations due within one year. Examples of short-term liabilities are payday loans and personal loans due within a year.

Payday loans are extremely short-term loans for a small amount of money. A person borrows money, usually at the highest interest rate allowed by law, until they receive a paycheck to pay the loan back. Every state has unique payday loan regulations. It is best to avoid this type of loan due to the extremely high interest and fees incurred.

Payday loans have HIGH interest rates!

Credit cards and other types of loans can be a short-term liability if the balance is required to be paid in full within a year. As is the case with short-term assets, a long-term liability can become a short-yerm liability once the paid-off date of the loan is within a year.

EXAMPLE 10

Suppose: Thomas obtained a five-year auto loan on March 15, 2010. If today is February 1, 2015, is his auto loan a short-term or long-term liability? Explain.

Answer: Thomas' auto loan is a short-term liability as of February 1, 2015, because his loan will mature, or be paid in full, within a year.

Some other types of short-term liabilities are not listed on a Personal Financial Statement (PFS). These include utility bills, cell phone bills, groceries, and clothing. Why aren't these included? A PFS is a personal balance sheet. It shows an overview of overall financial health, and it deals exclusively with what is owned (assets), what is owed (liabilities), and the resulting net worth. While everyday expenses are owed, they can be changed by changing circumstances such as moving to a less expensive place or discontinuing or lessening the usage of an item. Additionally, if a consumer stops paying a utility bill or cell phone bill, the company will stop allowing the use until the person begins to pay, and no additional charges will be incurred except for late fees and penalties. This is different from a loan in that loans must be paid back regardless of use, non-use, or lack of payment.

Expenses such as utility bills, cell phone bills, groceries, and household items appear on a **Personal Cash Flow Statement** (PCFS). A PCFS measures all inflows (income) and outflows (expenses), illustrating the net cash flow for a period of time, usually a month. This statement is useful when creating a budget and tracking a spending history.

EXERCISE 10

True or False:

1. True or False. Payday loans are a wise choice.

2. True or False. A short-term liability is a debt due within two years.

3. True or False. Living expenses are included Personal Financial Statements.

4. True or False. What is owed and owned is list on a PFS.

5. True or False. A PCFS measures all of the cash inflows and outflows for a given period of time, usually a month.

6. True or False. Short-term liabilities are also known as current liabilities.

Multiple Choice Problems:

7. If a person would like to know their net cash flow for a particular month, which one of the following would they use:

    a. Personal Financial Statement
    b. Monthly Financial Statement
    c. Personal Cash Flow Statement
    d. Monthly Cash Flow Statement

8. Which of the following is NOT a short-term liability:

    a. Auto loan due in nine months.
    b. A house loan due in ten years.
    c. A personal loan due in six months.
    d. A payday loan

9. PCFS stands for:

    a. Personal Cash Flow Statement
    b. Professional Cash Flow Statement
    c. Personal Current Flow Statement
    d. Proficient Cash Flow Statement

10. Which of the following is true about a payday loan:

    a. A payday loan is usually a long-term loan.
    b. A person can take their time paying a payday back.
    c. A payday loan offers a great deal on interest rates.
    d. A payday loan must be paid back when a person receives their next paycheck.

LESSON 11 - LONG-TERM LIABILITIES

Long-term liabilities, also called noncurrent liabilities, are debt obligations due after a year or more. There are many types of long-term liabilities. Credit cards, personal loans for longer than a year, home equity lines of credit, home loans, auto loans, student loans, and loans on life insurance policies are all examples of long-term liabilities. Unpaid taxes can also be a long-term liability. Additionally, a medical bill that will not be fully paid within a year is classified as a noncurrent liability.

Credit card debt, personal loans, and personal lines of credit are usually classified as "Notes Payable to Banks and Others" on a PFS. Loans with regular payments (monthly, for example) are known as installment loans. The installment loans section of a PFS includes loans for recreational vehicles, boats, autos, airplanes, school, etc. Installment loans are usually classified as auto and other. The installment loans section for autos also includes lease agreements for cars. Home loans, which typically require a monthly payment, fall under "Mortgages on Real Estate." Many people have insurance policies that allow the insured person to borrow money from the policy; these are called "Loans on Life Insurance." It is best to talk with a licensed insurance agent about life insurance.

When completing a PFS, the amounts included are the balances on the loans, not the amount of the original loans. For example, a person may have taken out a loan three years ago for $5,000, but today the remaining balance on that loan is $500. The remaining obligation of the loan is known as the **outstanding balance** and is the sum entered onto a PFS for the debt obligation.

The situation when a person's income cannot meet, or pay for, their debt obligations, is known as being **overextended**. Income should always be larger than debt obligations. The larger the margin between the two, the easier it is to pay for the debt obligations and the less stress a person endures. While some monthly obligations such as cell phone bills and utilities are not included on a PFS, these monthly obligations should always be accounted for when determining how much debt to incur.

When completing a PCFS, the outstanding balance of a debt is not recorded, but the monthly debt payment along with the expenses is included. For example, if a person originally obtained an auto loan for $5,000 with a monthly payment of $125 and it currently has an outstanding balance of $1,000, the monthly payment is recorded as $125 on the PCFS, and the outstanding balance of $1,000 is listed in the "Installment Account (Auto)" section.

There are also liabilities known as contingent liabilities. **Contingent liabilities** are obligations that may occur in the future. In other words, a liability may or may not occur because it is contingent upon something happening. A contingent liability should not be listed unless it is highly probable it will happen. Additionally, if the contingent liability has any value, it would not be listed until the contingency is removed. An example of a contingent liability is a high school student who is planning to attend college. It is a high probably they are going to attend the college because they applied and have been accepted. However, their attendance is contingent on their ability to obtain a student loan. If they are approved for a student loan, the liability of college debt is no longer a contingent liability.

EXERCISE 11

True or False:

1. True or False. An outstanding balance is the original amount of the loan.

2. True of False. Unpaid taxes can be a long-term liability.

3. True or False. A house loan is classified as an installment loan.

4. True or False. Being overextended is a sign of good financial health.

5. True or False. Installment loans have regular payments.

6. True or False. A loan can be taken against certain types of insurance policies.

Multiple Choice Problems:

7. A person has a $3,000 personal loan with an outstanding balance of $700 and a monthly payment of $75. Which section is the debt recorded in on a PFS:

    a. Installment Account (Other)
    b. Notes Payable to Banks and Others
    c. Accounts Payable
    d. Other Liabilities

8. Long-Term liabilities are also known as:

    a. Forever liabilities
    b. Longstanding liabilities
    c. Noncurrent liabilities
    d. None of the above

9. Which of the following is not a long-term liability:

    a. A 15-year mortgage.
    b. A 5-year auto loan.
    c. A 24-month personal loan
    d. A payday loan

10. How is a person's net worth determined:

    a. Total assets minus total liabilities
    b. Total liabilities minus total assets
    c. Current assets minus current liabilities
    d. Current assets divided by current liabilities

LESSON 12 - LIABILITIES SECTION ON A PERSONAL FINANCIAL STATEMENT

As stated in previous lessons, personal net worth is calculated by taking total assets and subtracting total liabilities. Once your net worth is determined, other ratios can be completed to establish your financial health. Of course, if your net worth is negative, your financial health is not good, and you need some help. It is obvious that if your total assets are greater than your total liabilities, you would have enough assets to sell and pay all of your debt obligations.

Now it is time to learn how to complete the liability section of a PFS. The illustration below is the liability section of a PFS.

LIABILITIES	DOLLARS Round to the nearest whole dollar
17. Notes Payable to Financial Institutions and Others ...	$________
18. Installment Account (Auto) ...	$________
19. Installment Account (Other) ...	$________
20. Loan on Life Insurance ...	$________
21. Mortgages on Real Estate ...	$________
22. Unpaid Taxes ...	$________
23. Other Liabilities ...	$________
24. Total	$________
25. Net Worth	$________

Each line in the table above is explained below and in Lesson 11.

Notes Payable to Banks and Others – Credit cards, personal loans, and personal lines of credit.

Installment Account (Auto) – includes all outstanding balances for all auto loans, which would include loans for boats, recreational vehicles, airplanes, etc.

Installment Account (Other) – includes student loans or other personal loans.

Mortgages on Real Estates – outstanding balance for all mortgages.

Unpaid Taxes – contains unpaid taxes that will not be paid within a year.

Other Liabilities – this category is for any debt obligations that do not fit into any of the other categories.

Net Worth - the difference between total assets and total liabilities

EXERCISE 12

Using the list of liabilities below, complete the liability table.

Caleb has the following liabilities.

- He owes $10,000 for a student loan.
- He owes $1,000 on a personal loan to a friend.
- The outstanding balance on his farm loan is $15,000.
- His life insurance policy has a value of $200,000, but he doesn't have a loan on it.
- He doesn't have any other debt obligations.
- He has an outstanding balance of $9,000 for his car.
- His credit card balance is $750.
- His motorcycle loan has a remaining balance of $900 due in six months.
- His house loan debt is $80,000.
- His taxes are paid up to date.

LIABILITIES	DOLLARS Round to the nearest whole dollar
1. Notes Payable to Financial Institutions and Others ...	$__________
2. Installment Account (Auto) ...	$__________
3. Installment Account (Other) ...	$__________
4. Loan on Life Insurance ...	$__________
5. Mortgages on Real Estate ...	$__________
6. Unpaid Taxes ...	$__________
7. Other Liabilities ...	$__________
8. Total	$__________

QUIZ - SECTION 3

Multiple Choice Problems:

1. Rebecca has an outstanding balance of $35,250 for all of her debt obligations and her total assets are $98,570. What is her debt ratio: (Round to nearest whole number with no decimals.)

    a. 35%
    b. 38%
    c. 36%
    d. 34%

2. Bill and Heather promised their 15-year-old teen they would pay for his/her college tuition; however, their teen doesn't know if he/she wants to attend college. What type of liability would Bill and Heather have:

    a. Current Liability
    b. Contingent Liability
    c. Noncurrent Liability
    d. It isn't a liability since their teen isn't sure they will attend college.

3. Brian's original auto loan was $8,250 and today he owes $4,365. What is his outstanding balance:

    a. $4,365
    b. $8,250
    c. $12,615
    d. $3,885

4. If Henry's total assets are $126,358 and his total liabilities are $76,406, what is his net worth:

    a. $126,358
    b. $76,406
    c. $49,952
    d. $202,764

5. When are short-term liabilities due:

    a. Short-term liabilities are due after a year or more.
    b. Short-term liabilities are due within a year.
    c. Short-term liabilities are due when the person feels like paying them.
    d. Short-term liabilities are due within 18 months.

Using the list of assets and liabilities on the left, answer questions 7 through 25 in the Assets and Liabilities Table.

Caleb has the following assets and liabilities. He didn't have time to sort them into categories, so the they are intermingled.

- $5,000 in stocks.
- Outstanding balance of $7,890 for my truck.
- $1,000 loan on my life insurance policy.
- Truck is worth $9,550.
- I owe $124,589 for my house.
- Three $2,500 CDs.
- Personal property is worth $5,000.
- $12,500 in student loan debt.
- $1,500 loan to my sister.
- Motorcycle is worth $5,000.
- All taxes are paid up-to-date.
- House appraised at $150,000.
- I opened an IRA with $10,000.
- Boat loan for $4,260
- Motorcycle only has $1,000 left on the loan.
- Antiques worth $6,000.
- There is $5,645 in my checking account.
- $75 cash at home.
- I have a 401k at work for $40,000.
- $2,000 in a savings account.
- Two credit cards with total balance of $2,300

ASSETS	DOLLARS Round to the nearest whole dollar
6. Cash on Hand at Financial institutions	$ ____________
7. Savings Accounts	$ ____________
8. IRA or Other Retirement Accounts	$ ____________
9. Accounts & Notes Receivable	$ ____________
10. Life Insurance - Cash Surrender Value Only ..	$ ____________
11. Stocks and Bonds	$ ____________
12. Real Estate	$ ____________
13. Automobile Present Value	$ ____________
14. Other - Personal Property	$ ____________
15. Other Assets	$ ____________
16. Total Assets	$ ____________
LIABILITIES	**DOLLARS** Round to the nearest whole dollar
17. Notes Payable to Financial Institutions and Others ...	$ ____________
18. Installment Account (Auto)	$ ____________
19. Installment Account (Other)	$ ____________
20. Loan on Life Insurance	$ ____________
21. Mortgages on Real Estate	$ ____________
22. Unpaid Taxes	$ ____________
23. Other Liabilities	$ ____________
24. Total Liabilities	$ ____________
25. Net Worth	$ ____________

SECTION 4 - WAGES

KEYWORDS

Benefits

Commissions

Dependents

Direct deposit

Exempt wages

Gross wage

Net wages

LEARNING OBJECTIVES FOR SECTION 4

Upon successful completion of Section 4, you will be able to:

- Explain the difference between gross and net wages.
- Understand types of wage withholdings.

LESSON 13 - GROSS WAGES

A **gross wage** is the monetary funds earned by an employee in exchange for work completed and can be earned in various ways. You can earn wages in various ways such as from a fixed amount per hour, tips, pay per job such as mowing a neighbor's lawn or babysitting, base pay or salary, overtime, bonuses, commissions, profit sharing, merit pay, and stock options.

An employee earns overtime pay once they have worked more than 40 hours in a workweek. This means the employee can work four 10-hour days or three 12-hour days in a given workweek and still not earn overtime pay. In other words, the 40-hour guideline is based on hours worked in a workweek, not the number of hours worked in a day. Overtime pay is 1 ½ times a person's hourly wage. For example, if you earned $10 an hour as your regular pay, your overtime pay would be $15 an hour, which is (10/2) + 10 = $15

The United States Department of Labor (DOL) has a minimum wage per hour amount that all employers in all states must follow; however, many states enact their own minimum wage that either meets or exceeds the DOL's minimum wage requirement. The Department of Labor uses the Fair Labor Standards Act (FLSA) to enforce the minimum wage and overtime pay standards.

Non-exempt employees get paid for overtime, exempt employees do not!

Employees who earn a salary, rather than a wage per hour, do not earn overtime pay. Salary is a fixed annual wage typically paid monthly or biweekly and is considered exempt. **Exempt wages** mean the employee is excluded from the overtime pay requirement. It is assumed the employer is paying a higher wage in exchange for employees working more than 40 hours in a workweek. Employees who receive a salary usually have significant experience and/or education in the particular field.

Commissions are earned either in addition to a base pay or without a base pay. Commissions are either a percentage or flat fee paid to an employee for each good or service sold. A commission scale is determined before the employee begins work. For example, if you worked for an auto dealer, you may earn a 10% commission for each car you sell. If the company makes a net profit of $5,000 for a car, you would then earn $500 as your commission. If you earned a flat fee for each car sold, you would receive the predetermined commission amount regardless of how much the company earns.

Benefits from an employer are considered part of the employee's pay package. Benefits are not typically paid to part-time employees; however, many employers do offer a condensed benefit package to their part-time employees. The monetary value of the benefits package cannot be calculated into the minimum wage, but many employers use the total of wages and benefits as the real cost of hiring an employee. Benefits can include medical and dental insurance, life insurance, vacation pay, severance pay, retirement, taxes, and jury duty pay. Many employers help keep the cost of medical and dental insurance lower for employees by paying a portion for the employee through group insurance rates.

EXERCISE 13

Multiple Choice Problems:

1. Which department of the United States sets the minimum wage:
   a. United States Department of Wages
   b. United States Department of Salaries
   c. United States Department of Labor
   d. United States Department of Income

2. Which of the following Act enforces the minimum wage:
   a. Fair Labor Standards Act
   b. Fair Working Standards Act
   c. Sarbanes-Oxley Act of 2002
   d. Fair Labor Ethics Act

3. Which of the following types of pay is considered exempt from overtime pay:
   a. Bonuses
   b. Hourly
   c. Salary
   d. Merit

4. Which of the following is true about commissions:
   a. All employees are entitled to receiving commissions for their work.
   b. Commissions are paid either as a percentage or a flat fee for a good or product sold.
   c. Commissions are the sum of money earned for overtime work.
   d. Commissions are not allowed in some states.

5. Which of the following defines gross wages:
   a. Gross wages are the monetary funds earned by an employer for work assigned.
   b. Gross wages are the benefits given to an employee by an employer.
   c. Gross wages are the monetary funds paid to employee after all deductions are subtracted.
   d. Gross wages are the monetary funds earned by an employee in exchange for work completed.

6. Which of the following describes overtime pay:
   a. Overtime pay is when an employee works more than 8 hours in a day.
   b. Overtime pay is when an employee works more than 40 hours in a workweek.
   c. Overtime pay is paid as a percentage of an employee's sales.
   d. Overtime pay is based on the total number of hours worked in a given day.

7. Which of the following is true about benefits:
   a. Benefits are considered part of employee's complete pay package.
   b. Most employers don't give any benefits to employees.
   c. All part-time employees receive benefits.
   d. Salaried employees don't get benefits.

8. Which of the following is an example of a benefit paid by an employer:
    a. Medical and dental insurance
    b. Vacation pay
    c. Retirement
    d. All of the above are examples of benefits paid by an employer.

9. Which of the following statements is true:
    a. States can choose to pay less than the federally mandated minimum.
    b. The Department of Labor does not set a minimum wage.
    c. States can choose to pay a minimum that meets or exceeds the federally mandated minimum wage.
    d. All states have to pay the same minimum wage to their employees.

10. If Charlie earns $20 per hour as his regular pay, how much would he earn per hour for overtime hours:
    a. $25
    b. $30
    c. $20
    d. $35

LESSON 14 - DEDUCTIONS ~ PART I (TAXES, INSURANCE)

Once an employee has earned gross wages, and before the employer can give the employee those earned wages, deductions must be applied. Deductions can be made for a number of reasons, but this discussion focuses on taxes, insurance, retirement, and garnishments. This lesson will discuss deductions for taxes and insurance. Lesson 15 will discuss retirement and garnishment wages.

Deductions are considered either mandatory or voluntary. Taxes are mandatory while insurance deductions are voluntary. Payroll taxes consist of Federal Tax (withholding), State and Local Tax (withholding), Social Security Tax (also known as FICA), and Medicare Tax. Insurance deductions can include health; dental; vision; accident, dismemberment, and disability (AD&D); and life insurance.

Various factors affect an individual's Federal Withholding amount including wage rate, number of dependents, marital status, pay frequency, and timing of deductions. The higher the wage rate, the higher the Federal withholding. The IRS has tables that show the percentage of gross wages deducted. Since this changes often, it is best to look at the tables online at https://www.irs.gov/payments/tax-withholding.

A **dependent** is a qualifying child or relative as defined by the IRS. There is a test to help a taxpayer determine if a child or relative qualifies as a dependent. Two important factors when claiming a dependent are (1) no one else is claiming that individual as their dependent, and (2) the individual relied on the person claiming them for their support for more than half of a given year. Marital status also affects the Federal Withholding rate and is included in the tables provided by the IRS.

Pay frequency has an impact on Federal withholding as well. If an individual is paid on a monthly basis they could potentially jump to the next, higher tax bracket with a larger amount of money withheld; whereas, if that person is paid once a week, they might be in a lower tax bracket because a lower amount being is withheld. Because the Federal withholding amount can change based on the gross wages for a particular paycheck, many companies pay bonuses in a separate paycheck to lessen the impact of the Federal Withholding on bonus pay.

The timing of certain deductions can also have an impact on gross wages. Several deductions, such as premiums for certain qualifying retirement plans, are deducted from gross wages before the Federal Withholding is calculated, so the employee does not pay tax on the retirement deduction amount.

Other tax withholdings are Social Security and Medicare Tax. Both the employer and employee pay these taxes. The Social Security tax rate has been 6.2% for both the employee and the employer since 1990. However, once an employee and employer has reached the earnings cap threshold and paid the social security tax on a particular dollar amount (the amount changes each year), this tax is no longer applied for the remainder of the year. For 2016, the earnings cap was $118,500. The Medicare tax rate for both employer and employee in 2016 is 1.45%; however, high-income earners (as defined by the IRS each year) pay an additional 0.9%. Self-employed taxpayers pay both the employer and employee rates. For example, a self-employed taxpayer pays 12.4% (6.2% employee + 6.2% employer) for the Social Security tax (FICA) and 2.9% (1.45% employee + 1.45% employer) for the Medicare tax.

EXAMPLE 14

Suppose: Clarence reached the $118,500 earnings cap threshold for the Social Security tax for 2016. Would he pay Social Security tax in his next paycheck? Explain. When would he begin to pay Social Security tax again?

Answer: No, once Clarence reaches the $118,500 earnings limit for Social Security tax for 2016, he would no longer pay Social Security tax for 2016. Clarence would begin to pay Social Security tax at the beginning of the next calendar year, which would be 2017 in this example.

State and Local (city and/or county) taxes vary by state, city, and county. In fact, in some states, cities, and counties, employees do not have to pay any state or local taxes. If a taxpayer is interested in knowing if they pay state and local taxes, they can look on their paycheck stub as all deductions are itemized. Worker's Compensation (WC) is insurance paid by employers. WC pays wages and medical benefits to employees when they have been injured on the job. Employees can obtain specific details about WC from the Human Resource Department or supervisor at their company.

As mentioned earlier, an employee may opt to carry various types of insurance which result in voluntary deductions. If an individual is covered by their parents', spouse's, or another individual's health insurance policy they can waive the health insurance offered by their employer; however, with the new Affordable Care Act, it is important to ask the employer the new rules when deciding on medical insurance options. While health insurance is offered by most companies, dental and vision insurance is not. Some companies offer these two types of add-on insurances and others do not.

Many companies pay a portion of the health insurance (and dental and vision when offered) monthly premiums for employees. For example, if the monthly premium for a single person is $150, the company might pay $75 and the employee might pay the other half. Other types of insurance policies offered are AD&D and life insurance. These are usually at very low rates.

Group insurance rates through an employer are usually lower than the rate a person obtains on their own. When insurance is provided through an employer, premiums are deducted from the participating employee's gross wages before taxes, which means less taxes are paid.

EXERCISE 14

Multiple Choice Problems:

1. Which of the following is not an example of a tax withheld from gross wages:
    a. Federal Tax
    b. State Tax
    c. Property Tax
    d. Medicare Tax

2. Which of the following is not an example of a Federal Tax:
    a. Federal Tax
    b. State Tax
    c. Social Security Tax
    d. Medicare Tax

3. Social Security tax is paid on gross wages up to which of the following dollar amounts for 2016:
    a. $118,000
    b. $117,500
    c. $117,000
    d. $118,500

4. Which of the following is true:
    a. The employer pays the same Social Security and Medicare tax rate on an employee's gross wages.
    b. The employer pays a ¼ of what the employee pays for social security and Medicare tax.
    c. The employer only pays the Social Security tax and the employee only pays the Medicare tax.
    d. The employer only pays the Medicare tax and the employee only pays the Social Security tax.

5. The tax rate for each the employer and the employee for Social Security taxes is:
    a. 6.2%
    b. 12.4%
    c. 1.45%
    d. 2.9%

6. The tax rate for each the employer and the employee for Medicare taxes is:
    a. 6.2%
    b. 12.4%
    c. 1.45%
    d. 2.9%

7. High-income earners, as defined by the IRS, pays an additional:
    a. 0.10%
    b. 0.95%
    c. 2.9%
    d. 0.9%

8. Which of the following is true:
    a. Companies do not contribute any money toward health insurance premiums.
    b. Many companies contribute money towards health insurance premiums.
    c. All companies must pay for all health insurance premiums.
    d. All employees must accept health insurance from their employers even if they already have health insurance.

9. Which of the following is a true statement:
    a. Only some people pay Federal Withholdings.
    b. Only some employers pay Federal Withholdings.
    c. The timing of certain deductions can have an effect the Federal tax deduction.
    d. The timing of certain deductions never has an effect on the Federal tax deduction.

10. Which of the following is a true statement:
    a. Some states do not have income taxes.
    b. Every state has income taxes.
    c. Some years the government doesn't charge any Federal taxes.
    d. Employees only begin to pay Federal taxes once they hit a certain gross wage.

LESSON 15- DEDUCTIONS ~ PART II (RETIREMENT, GARNISHMENTS)

Two other types of deductions are retirement and garnishments. Retirement plans can be government sponsored, personal, or employer sponsored. The most well-known government sponsored retirement plan is Social Security. Aside from Social Security, other government sponsored retirement plans are typically for government employees.

The most well-known employer sponsored retirement plan is the 401K. Many employers will make a matching contribution to the plan up to a certain percentage of the employee's salary. Other popular employer sponsored retirement plans are profit-sharing, defined benefit pension plans, and Roth 401(k). Research these plans online for detailed information.

For personal retirement plans, an established amount is deducted from an employee's paycheck and deposited directly into the plan. These are usually IRAs, annuities, or interest-bearing savings accounts.

Garnishments occur when a court orders money to be deducted from the wages of an employee for unpaid debts. Garnishments, however, are not the same as income deduction orders. Garnishments have limits. First, a creditor has to obtain a judgment against the employee with the delinquent debt. Then, there are federal limits on how much can be garnished. This limit is the lesser of 25% of disposable income (gross wages minus deductions) or the amount of wages that exceeds 30 times the federal minimum wage. Some states apply wage garnishment laws that are stricter than the federal wage garnishment laws.

Unpaid debts can be garnished from wages.

An income deduction order is issued by the court and is like a garnishment in that it is used to deduct money from an employee's wages for debt obligations; however, an income deduction order is mainly used for Chapter 13 bankruptcies and child support. Other differences between an income deduction order and a garnishment are that income deduction orders are not always limited in how much can be deducted. In addition, income deduction orders may be issued when an employee is not behind on payments. For example, if the employee has filed a Chapter 13 bankruptcy, also known as a wage earner plan, they have created a repayment plan to pay all or some of their outstanding debt to their creditors. Once this plan is approved by the court, an order for the agreed upon monthly payment may be issued to their employer for a mandatory deduction. This ensures the employee follows the plan. An income deduction order is sometimes put in place for child support for the same reasons.

EXERCISE 15

Multiple Choice Problems:

1. Which of the following is not an example of a retirement deduction:
    a. 401(k)
    b. Profit-sharing
    c. Child support
    d. IRA

2. Retirement plans can be all of the following except:
    a. Government sponsored
    b. Employer sponsored
    c. Personal
    d. All of the above are correct

3. An income deduction order is:
    a. Issued by the court.
    b. Issued by the employer.
    c. Issued by the employee.
    d. None of the above are correct.

4. Which of the following is an example of a wage garnishment limit:
    a. The lesser of 25% of disposal income or the amount of wages that exceeds 30 times the federal minimum wage.
    b. The lesser of 25% of wages that exceeds 30 times the federal minimum wage and 30 times of disposal income.
    c. There is no limit for wage garnishments.
    d. Companies decide how much to garnish employee wages.

5. Which of the following types of bankruptcies is used to create a payment plan to payback creditors:
    a. Chapter 7
    b. Chapter 11
    c. Chapter 8
    d. Chapter 13

6. Which of the following is one of the most popular types of government sponsored retirement plans?
    a. 401(k)
    b. Social Security
    c. Annuity deposits
    d. Income deduction plan

7. A Chapter 13 bankruptcy is also known as:
    a. Income deduction plan
    b. A garnishment plan
    c. A delinquent debt plan
    d. A wage earner plan

8. An income deduction order is typically used for:
    a. Outstanding mortgage loan
    b. Any and all loans in default
    c. Chapter 13 bankruptcies and child support payments
    d. Credit card debt.

9. Which of the following is true:
    a. States can set stricter wage garnishment limits than the federal government.
    b. States cannot set any wage garnishment limits.
    c. States can remove federal government wage garnishment limits.
    d. States can set less strict wage garnishment limits than the federal government.

10. Creditors (which is true):
    a. can garnish wages without a judgment from the courts.
    b. must obtain a judgment from the courts to garnish wages.
    c. never garnish wages for unpaid debt.
    d. set the wage garnishment limits.

LESSON 16 - NET WAGES

Most companies use direct deposit to pay wages to employees.

did you KNOW?

Once an employer subtracts all deductions from an employee's gross wages, the resulting amount is the net wages paid to the employee. A net wage is also commonly known as net pay and take-home pay. Wages are usually paid either by a check or direct deposit into the employee's savings or checking account. Most employers prefer paying through direct deposit; however, person's 17 years old or younger cannot open a savings or checking account at a financial institution without an adult as an additional account holder. Opening an account with a financial institution requires the account holder to sign a contract and minors cannot legally enter into a contract.

Having savings or checking accounts helps with money management. However, if finding an adult to sign onto an account is not possible, a minor employee can request a paper check as direct deposit is not mandatory and cannot be forced.

There are many sites to help calculate net pay. An online paycheck calculator will probably not be exact, but it will be a good estimate. Companies have different pay frequency. Pay frequencies can be daily, weekly, bi-weekly, semi-monthly, monthly, quarterly, semi-annually, and annually. The most popular pay frequencies are weekly, bi-weekly, semi-monthly, and monthly.

EXAMPLE 16-1

Suppose: Joy works full-time. Her hourly wage is $10 per hour, and she lives in Missouri. She is single and does not claim any federal allowances/deductions and has no exemptions. She is paid bi-weekly. Her taxes are as follows: Federal - $89.18, FICA (Social Security) - $49.60, Medicare - $11.60, and State - $19.00. She has no other deductions. What are her gross wages, total deductions, and net pay?

Answer: Her gross wages are $800.00, her total deductions are $169.38, and her net pay is $630.62 (800.00 – 169.38).

EXAMPLE 16-2

Suppose: Amber works full-time. Her hourly wage is $12 per hour and she lives in Texas. She is single and does not claim any federal allowances or deductions and has no exemptions. She gets paid bi-weekly. Her taxes are as follows: Federal - $113.18, FICA (Social Security) - $59.52, Medicare - $13.92, and State - $0.00. She also has a health insurance deduction of $48.00. What are her gross wages, total deductions, and net pay?

Answer: Her gross wages are $960.00, her total deductions are $234.62, and her net pay is $725.38 (960.00 – 234.62).

EXERCISE 16

Questions 1 – 5 are based on the following information.

Sherri is single and works full-time at ZYX Company in New Mexico. The following is information to calculate her next paycheck:

ITEM	AMOUNT	ITEM	AMOUNT
Hourly pay rate	15.00	Exemptions	1
Pay frequency	Bi-Weekly	Hours worked each week	48
Deductions:			
Federal	172.80	FICA	96.72
Medicare	22.62	State	51.52
Workman's Comp.	0.31	Health Insurance	50.00
401k	46.80		

1. What is Sherri's gross pay? (Don't forget about overtime pay).
   a. $1,440
   b. $1,560
   c. $1,400
   d. $1,500

2. How much are Sherri's total deductions?
   a. $440.77
   b. $400.00
   c. $390.77
   d. $172.80

3. How much is Sherri's Worker's Compensation deduction?
   a. $22.62
   b. $51.52
   c. $22.93
   d. $0.31

4. How much is Sherri's Social Security deduction?
   a. $0.31
   b. $22.62
   c. $96.72
   d. $172.80

5. How much is Sherri's take home pay?
   a. $1,119.54
   b. $1,119.23
   c. $1,166.03
   d. $1,166.34

QUIZ - SECTION 4

True or False:

1. True or False. Gross wages are the same as take home pay.

2. True or False. WC stands for Worker's Compensation.

3. True or False. Garnishments can occur without a court order.

4. True or False. Net pay is what the employee is given after all deductions are subtracted from gross wages.

5. True or False. Overtime pay is based on the number of hours worked in a given day.

6. True or False. Deductions are considered either mandatory or voluntary.

7. True or False. An income deduction order is for delinquent payments for medical bills.

8. True or False. All employees must agree to direct deposit in order to receive their net pay.

9. True or False. States can set a higher minimum wage than the federal minimum wage.

10. True or False. Social Security is a government sponsored retirement plan.

Multiple Choice Problems:

11. Which of the following governmental entities sets the federal minimum Wage:
    a. Department of Labor
    b. Internal Revenue Service
    c. Fair Labor Standards Act
    d. Department of Wage & Labor

12. The federal withholding rate can be found:
    a. at the Security of State's office.
    b. at the unemployment office.
    c. at the IRS website.
    d. at the City Clerk's office.

13. Which of the following is true about garnishments:
    a. Garnishments are the same as income deduction orders.
    b. Garnishments must be ordered by a court.
    c. Garnishments do not need to be ordered by a court.
    d. Garnishments are decided by the employer.

14. Net pay is (pick the statement that is correct):
    a. the monetary funds earned by an employee before deductions.
    b. half of the gross wages.
    c. the same as gross wages.
    d. the take home pay after all deductions are subtracted from gross wages.
15. Benefits to employees (pick the statement that is correct):
    a. are always paid to part-time employees.
    b. must include a free lunch every day.
    c. must include a retirement plan.
    d. are considered part of a person's pay package.

16. Which of the following is true about pay frequency:
    a. It is how often an employee is paid.
    b. It is how often an employee works to earn pay.
    c. It has not impact on the federal withholding amount.
    d. It includes employees who get paid every two years.

17. An income deduction is which of the following:
    a. Issued by the court typically for all outstanding loans.
    b. Issued by the court typically for Chapter 13 Bankruptcies and child support.
    c. Issued by the employer typically for all outstanding loans.
    d. Issued by the employer typically for Chapter 13 Bankruptcies and child support.

18. Which of the following is true about retirement plans?
    a. All employers offer a retirement plan to their employees.
    b. Only the government offers a retirement plan to workers.
    c. Employees have to be 25 years of age to start a retirement plan.
    d. A personal retirement plan can be start by an employee.

19. Which federal governmental entity enforces the minimum wage?
    a. Department of Labor
    b. Internal Revenue Service
    c. Fair Labor Standards Act
    d. Department of Wage & Labor

20. Deductions can include which of the following?
    a. FICA
    b. State and local taxes
    c. Medicare tax
    d. All of the above

Questions 21 – 25 are based on the following information.

Chuck is single and works full-time at ABC Company in California. The following is information to calculate his next paycheck:

ITEM	AMOUNT	ITEM	AMOUNT
Hourly pay rate	20.00	Exemptions	1
Pay frequency	Bi-Weekly	Hours worked each week	50
Deductions:			
Federal	310.28	FICA	136.40
Medicare	31.90	State	95.68
Workman's Comp.	19.80	Health Insurance	50.00
401k	66.00		

21. What is Chuck's gross pay? (Don't forget about overtime pay).
    a. $2,200
    b. $2,000
    c. $2,500
    d. $1,600

22. How much are Chuck's total deductions?
    a. $310.28
    b. $779.86
    c. $710.06
    d. $736.40

23. How much is Chuck's Disability Insurance deduction?
    a. $31.90
    b. $19.80
    c. $51.70
    d. $66.00

24. How much is Chuck's Social Security deduction?
    a. $19.80
    b. $136.40
    c. $95.68
    d. $31.90

25. How much is Chuck's take home pay?
    a. $1,490.94
    b. $1,489.50
    c. $1,490.94
    d. $1,489.94

SECTION 5 - PERSONAL FINANCIAL STATEMENT

LEARNING OBJECTIVES FOR SECTION 5

Upon successful completion of Section 5, you will be able to:

- Complete a personal financial statement.

LESSON 17 - INTRO TO A PFS - CASE STUDY I ~ 25 YEARS OLD

Everyone goes through financial phases during life. When beginning adult life (early 20's) most people do not have as much in assets or liabilities as they do later when in their 40's. Later, nearing retirement, most people tend to have fewer liabilities and more assets. Now, it is time to apply information learned in Sections 1 through 4 to three case studies. These case studies will illustrate where some people tend to be in their financial path in their mid-20's, 40's, and 60's. The case studies will pull all of the previous information together and apply it to completing Personal Financial Statements (PFS).

PFSs are required by some financial institutions when a loan is requested. These documents are typically two to six pages in length and are a longer version of a personal asset and liability table. The additional pages provide areas for listing assets and liabilities individually.

The first page of a PFS has space for adding contact information and for listing assets, liabilities, contingent liabilities, and net worth. As discussed in previous lessons, assets and liabilities can be sorted into categories. On a PFS, contingent liabilities are listed in a separate area; in a basic net worth calculation, contingent liabilities are not usually listed. In the sources of income section on a PFS, income is listed as the annual income because the remainder of the PFS is based on annual figures. It is important to remain consistent when completing financial information. All of the information should contain the same time period (e.g. monthly, quarterly, or annually). PFSs typically look at finances of an annual basis.

Longer PFSs require itemization of the information on the first page by listing assets and liabilities individually on the remaining pages. For example, if a perspective borrower has two vehicle loans, the loans would be combined in the outstanding loan balance on the first page in the liability section, but the vehicles would be listed individually on the second page in the designated area. When listing the vehicles individually, additional information about the loans is requested. This includes monthly loan payment, term of the loan (number of months for the loan), beginning loan amount, outstanding balance, and start and maturity dates. For our purposes, we will be working with a typical first page of a PFS only.

These case studies will follow one fictitious person's financial path throughout their life. We will start with their life when they are 25 years old, then revisit them on their financial path when they are 45 years old, and finish up by visiting their financial path when they are 65-years old. Life continues well beyond 65 years of age; however, these case studies demonstrate the natural progression of a typical person's financial path throughout life and allow you some hands-on practice.

Case Study I - 25 Years' Old

We begin with David Jones who is now 25. David graduated from college two years ago with $30,000 in student loan debt. Since his graduation, he purchased a vehicle. David traded in the car he used throughout his college days, but he also owns a motorcycle. Additionally, he incurred some credit card debt when he needed furniture.

David is not married yet, but he will soon marry Becky. He has some pending financial obligations for the wedding: the wedding photographer and the honeymoon expenses. David and Becky have already paid for many of the other wedding expenses, and Becky's family is paying for the remainder of the wedding. David currently leases an apartment that will accommodate the couple after the wedding. They plan to wait to buy a house.

EXERCISE 17

Take a look at all of the David's income, assets, liabilities, and personal information. Then complete the Personal Financial Statement for David. David lives at 1234 Path Lane, Charleston, SC 29401. He does not have a home phone and his cell phone is 843-555-1234. He works at ABC Company and makes $28,000 a year.

Cash - $200
Wedding photo impending cost - $1,000
Car value - $17,000
Personal property - $5,000
Student loans - $30,000
Savings account - $6,000
Motorcycle value - $8,000
Credit Card - $2,000
Honeymoon impending cost - $4,000
Car loan - $12,000
Loan to his brother - $3,000
Checking account - $2,500

Use the information above and complete a PFS for David. Use today's date for the date.

PERSONAL FINANCIAL STATEMENT

1	Date		
2	Name	Home #	5
3	Address	Cell #	6
4	City, State, & Zip Code		

	ASSETS		LIABILITIES		
7	Cash on hand & in Financial Institutions		Notes Payable to Financial Inst. & Others		22
8	Savings Account		Installment Account (Auto)		23
9	IRA or Other Retirement Account		Installment Account (Other)'		24
10	Accounts & Notes Receivable		Loan on Life Insurance		25
11	Life Insurance - Cash Surrender Value Only		Mortgages on Real Estate		26
12	Stocks and Bonds		Unpaid Taxes		27
13	Real Estate		Other Liabilities		28
14	Automobile - Present Value				
15	Other - Personal Property				
16	Other Assets		**Total Liabilities**		29
17	**Total Assets**		**Net Worth**		30
	Sources of Income		**Contingent Liabilities**		
18					31
19					32
20					33
21					34

LESSON 18 - CASE STUDY II ~ 45 YEARS OLD

We continue with David Jones' financial path journey in this lesson. David married Becky and they have two children. Their son, John, will graduate from high school this year and is looking at colleges, but there is a chance he might change his mind to take advantage of a job offer. Their other child, Lizzie, has three years until she graduates high school.

David's life and financial path has changed significantly since he was 25 years old. Also, his assets and liabilities have seen major fluctuations. This is quite normal. David and Becky have worked hard to save money, and they have endured many obstacles along their financial path. Many adults come upon financial situations where they have to decide which course of action to take, and David, Becky, and their son, John, are in one of those situations.

John is considering attending Clemson University to work towards a degree in forestry in the fall; however, he has spent his high school summers working for his uncle's logging company and loves that work. His uncle offered John a job at the logging company to begin when he graduates from high school. David and Becky want to help John with his college tuition, but they are not in a position to pay all of it. Clemson's estimated cost for college in 2016 for one year is $27,890. John has been awarded $10,000 in scholarships and grants, bringing the costs down to $17,890. After the summer, John will have $10,000 saved from working with the logging company. David and Becky are debating whether they can help John with the other $7,890 if he decides to attend Clemson.

It is currently February. In order to decide where they might obtain the $7,890 to help John, David and Becky decide to create a Personal Financial Statement to analyze their financial situation. Look at David's and Becky's income, assets, liabilities, and personal information in Exercise 18.1 to help determine what they should do. They will consider using their money in savings, taking a loan against David's life insurance, cashing in their stocks or CDs, or possibly borrowing money.

EXERCISE 18.1

David and Becky now live at 5678 Holler Lane, Charleston, SC 29401. They do not have a home phone and their contact cell phone is 843-555-7777. David works at MNO Company and makes $78,000 a year and Becky works part-time and makes $20,000 annually.

Cash - $300	Car #1 value - $22,000	Credit Card - $8,000
Pending college costs - $7,890	Jewelry - $20,000	RV Loan - $6,000
Car #2 value - $9,000	House value - $150,000	RV Value - $9,000
Personal property - $15,000	Car #1 loan - $15,000	Antiques - $6,000
Retirement - $80,000	Mortgage - $112,500	Stocks - $10,000
Savings account - $12,000	Life Insurance Cash Value - $20,000	
Checking account - $1,500	CD that matures in 6 months - $6,000	

Use the information above and complete a PFS for David and Becky. Use February 27, 2016, as the date.

PERSONAL FINANCIAL STATEMENT

1	Date		
2	Name	Home #	5
3	Address	Cell #	6
4	City, State, & Zip Code		

	ASSETS		LIABILITIES		
7	Cash on hand & in Financial Institutions		Notes Payable to Financial Inst. & Others		22
8	Savings Account		Installment Account (Auto)		23
9	IRA or Other Retirement Account		Installment Account (Other)'		24
10	Accounts & Notes Receivable		Loan on Life Insurance		25
11	Life Insurance - Cash Surrender Value Only		Mortgages on Real Estate		26
12	Stocks and Bonds		Unpaid Taxes		27
13	Real Estate		Other Liabilities		28
14	Automobile - Present Value				
15	Other - Personal Property				
16	Other Assets		Total Liabilities		29
17	Total Assets		Net Worth		30
	Sources of Income		**Contingent Liabilities**		
18	Salary		As Signer		31
19	Net Investment Income		Legal Claims & Judgments		32
20	Real Estate Income		Other Special Debt		33
21	Other Income				

EXERCISE 18.2

Where might David and Becky obtain the $7,890 to help John if he decides to go to Clemson?

LESSON 19 - CASE STUDY III ~ 65 YEARS OLD

This is the final case study for David and Becky Jones. David is now 65 years old. David and Becky are looking forward to retirement in a few years. They have worked hard and hope to retire without debt.

They have considered downsizing their house, but they have grandchildren who visit often. For now, they will remain at the current residence until they both retire. Some people have debt they are paying off while in their mid-60s; others do not. Each person has a different financial path which varies according to the circumstances in their life.

While David and Becky have paid off most of their debt, they obtained a medical loan to pay for procedures both David and Becky have had in the past year. David and Becky love to go on trips in their RV; they use their vacation time to visit their children and grandchildren. They are considering traveling full-time with their RV when they retire in two or three years. Recently they traded the RV they used when John and Lizzie were teenagers for a new one.

David and Becky inherited some jewelry and antiques from their families. They plan to pass these items along to their children someday. They also invested in a small business venture several years ago from which they receive a monthly income. The business is still going strong, and they plan to keep their partnership interest in the business.

EXERCISE 19

David and Becky still live at 5678 Holler Lane, Charleston, SC 29401. They do not have a home phone and their contact cell phone is 843-555-7777. David works is still at MNO Company and he now makes $125,000 a year and Becky has been working full-time and makes $45,000 annually. They also receive $1,500 from their business venture each month.

Checking account - $3,500
Retirement - $500,000
House value - $230,000
Personal property - $25,000
Loan to John - $3,400
Life Insurance Cash Value - $32,000

Car #1 value - $15,000
Car #2 value - $12,000
RV Value - $45,000
CDs - $20,000
Savings account - $42,000

Jewelry - $35,000
Antiques - $30,000
Stocks - $28,000
RV loan - $20,000
Cash - $200

Use the information above and complete a PFS for David and Becky. Use today's date as the date.

PERSONAL FINANCIAL STATEMENT

1	Date		
2	Name	Home #	5
3	Address	Cell #	6
4	City, State, & Zip Code		

	ASSETS		LIABILITIES		
7	Cash on hand & in Financial Institutions		Notes Payable to Financial Inst. & Others		22
8	Savings Account		Installment Account (Auto)		23
9	IRA or Other Retirement Account		Installment Account (Other)'		24
10	Accounts & Notes Receivable		Loan on Life Insurance		25
11	Life Insurance - Cash Surrender Value Only		Mortgages on Real Estate		26
12	Stocks and Bonds		Unpaid Taxes		27
13	Real Estate		Other Liabilities		28
14	Automobile - Present Value				
15	Other - Personal Property				
16	Other Assets		**Total Liabilities**		29
17	**Total Assets**		**Net Worth**		30
	Sources of Income		**Contingent Liabilities**		
18	Salary		As Signer		31
19	Net Investment Income		Legal Claims & Judgments		32
20	Real Estate Income		Other Special Debt		33
21	Other Income				

QUIZ - SECTION 5

True or False:

1. True or False. Each person's financial situation remains stagnant over time.

2. True or False. People in their forties then to have more debt than people in their 60s.

3. True or False. A Personal Financial Statements allows a person to see their financial health.

4. True or False. Personal Financial Statements are often requested by financial institutions for small business loans.

5. True or False. There are many different types of Personal Financial Statements.

6. True or False. Personal Financial Statements only list current assets.

7. True or False. Contingent liabilities are never listed on a PFS.

8. True or False. A PFS requires a list of monthly expenses.

9. True or False. A PFS should be completed on an annual basis at a minimum.

10. True or False. A person really doesn't need to start creating an annual PFS until they are in their 40s.

UNIT 1 TEST

Multiple Choice Problems:

1. Which of the following is typically used by companies to identify the money made on their financial statements:
    a. Income
    b. Revenues
    c. Proceeds
    d. Takings

2. Which of the following explains earned income:
    a. It is money received from performing work or providing services.
    b. It is money received when work isn't performed or services provided.
    c. It is money received as a gift for a birthday.
    d. It is money received in exchange for a personal item.

3. Unearned income is defined as:
    a. It is money received from performing work or providing services.
    b. It is money received when work isn't performed or services provided.
    c. It is money received as a gift for a birthday.
    d. It is money received in exchange for a personal item.

4. Costs that do not change from month-to-month are:
    a. Variable expenses
    b. Discretionary expenses
    c. Fixed expenses
    d. None of these

5. Which of the following costs is an example of a discretionary expense:
    a. Eating out
    b. Utility expense
    c. Auto loan payment
    d. Rent payment

6. An expense that changes with a person income and/or activity is called a:
    a. Fixed expense
    b. Discretionary expense
    c. Monthly expense
    d. Variable expense

7. Which of the following is true about savings:
    a. Savings isn't really necessary.
    b. Savings is started later in life.
    c. Savings is putting money aside for use at some point in the future.
    d. None of the above are true.

8. The money paid by a company to their shareholders is called a:
    a. Dividend
    b. Interest
    c. Earned income
    d. Revenues

9. The date at the end of a term is referred to as a:
    a. Ending date
    b. Final date
    c. Maturity date
    d. Late date

10. Which of the following is an example of laddering:
    a. Opening several loans with staggered maturity dates.
    b. Opening several CDs with staggered maturity dates.
    c. Opening three savings accounts on different days.
    d. Having accounts at multiple financial institutions.

11. Giving is:
    a. freely giving something to someone with an expectation of something in return.
    b. giving something to someone by force
    c. loaning something to someone for a period of time.
    d. freely giving something to someone without an expectation of something in return.

12. Itemizing deductions is:
    a. listing all allowable deductions in order to lower one's taxable income.
    b. listing all allowable deductions in order to have for insurance.
    c. listing all allowable deductions is not necessary.
    d. None of these.

13. Personal net worth is calculated by:
    a. Subtracting total assets from total liabilities.
    b. Subtracting current liabilities from current assets.
    c. Subtracting total liabilities from total assets.
    d. Subtracting current assets from current liabilities.

14. Assets are item that are:
    a. Owed
    b. Owned
    c. Borrowed
    d. All of these

15. An item that can be moved from place to place is which of the following:
    a. Current asset
    b. Liability
    c. Appraisal
    d. Personal property

16. A(n) _______________ is when an expert gives an estimated value to property or goods.
    a. Estimated guess
    b. Conjecture
    c. Appraisal
    d. Speculation

17. Short-term assets are also known as:
    a. Current assets
    b. Existing assets
    c. Present assets
    d. Remaining assets

18. When something is paid for before it becomes due it is known as a:
    a. Prepaid asset
    b. Liability
    c. Future asset
    d. Impending asset

19. Which of the following is true:
    a. Tangible and intangible is the same thing.
    b. Tangible assets cannot be seen or identified by touch.
    c. Intangible assets cannot be seen or identified by touch.
    d. There is no such thing as an intangible asset.

20. Which of the following is an example of an intangible asset:
    a. Bicycle
    b. Copyright
    c. Automobile
    d. Jewelry

21. Long-term assets are:
    a. not permanent in nature and will be turned into cash within a year.
    b. permanent in nature and will be turned into cash within a year.
    c. not permanent in nature and will not be turned into cash within a year.
    d. permanent in nature and will not be turned into cash within a year.

22. A liability is something that is:
    a. Owed
    b. Owned
    c. Borrowed
    d. All of these

23. The value in property after all attached debts to the property have been subtracted is called:
    a. Liability
    b. Equity
    c. Asset
    d. Extra money

24. A current liability is also known as a:
    a. Current asset
    b. Long-term liability
    c. Short-term liability
    d. Equity

25. Which of the following is an example of a payday loan:
    a. A six-month loan
    b. A two-year loan
    c. A five-year loan
    d. A fifteen-day loan

26. A Personal Cash Flow Statement is used to:
    a. List monthly expenses and income.
    b. List all assets and liabilities
    c. List all debts coming due with a year
    d. None of these

27. A Personal Financial Statement is used to:
    a. List monthly expenses and income
    b. Measure the financial health for a person
    c. Isn't necessary to do
    d. All of the above

28. Long-term liabilities is a:
    a. Money that is due to a person within a year or more.
    b. Debt obligation that is due within a year or more.
    c. Debt obligation that is due after a year or more.
    d. Money that is due to a person after a year or more.

29. Loans with payments at regular intervals are known as:
    a. Monthly loans
    b. Long-term loans
    c. Regular payment loans
    d. Installment loans

30. Which of the following defines an outstanding balance on a loan:
    a. A balance that is incredible.
    b. The remaining obligation on a loan.
    c. Both a and b.
    d. Neither a or b.

31. When a person's income cannot meet their debt obligation it is known as being:
    a. Overextended
    b. Down on one's luck
    c. Overstretched
    d. Overreached

32. Obligations that are probably to occur in the future are called:
    a. Long-term liabilities
    b. Current liabilities
    c. Contingent liabilities
    d. Short-term liabilities

33. Gross wages are:
    a. Monetary funds earned by an employee in exchange for work completed.
    b. Monetary funds after all deductions.
    c. Monetary funds received a gift.
    d. Monetary funds received from an investment in stocks.

34. Monetary funds subtracted from gross wages are referred to as:
    a. Rewards
    b. Deductions
    c. Awards
    d. Net wages

35. Net wages is:
    a. Money earned from commissions.
    b. The money earned before any deductions.
    c. Money received as a bonus.
    d. The take home pay after all deductions.

UNIT 2
FINANCIAL TOOLS

Learning Objectives

Upon successful completion of this unit, you will be able to do the following:

- Apply basic financial theories to eveyday financial decisions.
- Differentiate between financial account types.
- Know how to open a checking and savings account.
- Reconcile a checking and savings account.
- Write a check.
- Explain types of investment tools.
- Differentiate between stocks, bonds, mutual funds, and other investments.
- Distinguish between a secured loan from an unsecured loan.
- Calculate a loan payment.
- Describe a creditor's loan approval process.
- Read and understand a credit report.
- Explain the components of a FICO Score.

SECTION 6 - BASIC FINANCIAL THEORIES

KEYWORDS

Cash

Compound interest

Debt

Future value or FV

House poor

Investment income

Present value or PV

Opportunity cost

Simple interest

Time value of money

LEARNING OBJECTIVES FOR SECTION 6

Upon successful completion of Section 6, you will be able to:

- Apply basic financial theories to eveyday financial decisions.

LESSON 20 - OPPORTUNITY COSTS

An **opportunity cost** is that which is lost when one opportunity is chosen over an alternative opportunity. You may think of opportunity cost as being related to money, but it can also be related to time, benefits, land, or anything of value to an individual. In other words, you can have two or more opportunities. When you chose one opportunity over another, you have to determine what benefits you will give up with the opportunity that is not chosen.

For example, Jacob has an opportunity to work a five-hour shift and make $10 per hour. He also has the opportunity to spend time hiking and eating lunch with friends during those same five hours. The hike and lunch will cost $25. If he chooses to go hiking, he will lose the opportunity to make $50. In other words, his opportunity cost is $50 for hiking and lunch with friends. He could choose to work and make $50 and spend time hiking and having lunch with those same friends on a different day.

The following are examples of opportunity costs:

- Buying trendy clothes instead of buying less expensive ones. The opportunity cost of buying expensive clothes is the money not saved when buying those clothes over buying the less expensive ones.

- Going to college instead working a full-time job. The opportunity cost in going to college is the money not earned by working full-time instead.

- Spending time with friends instead of studying for a test. The opportunity cost in spending time with friends is the knowledge not learned and/or retained for the test.

- Starting a business rather than working for a company. The opportunity cost in starting a business are the wages and benefits given up that could be earned from working for a company.

- Sleeping in one morning instead of getting chores completed. The opportunity cost of sleeping in may be the time forfeited later doing chores rather than spending time with friends.

What opportunity will be given up with your next big decision?

Opportunity costs exists in many decisions because most decisions mean giving up something in order to do something else. Decision making is not always easy because there are often advantages and disadvantages regardless of which opportunity is chosen. For example, while you might give up the opportunity to make money if you attend college, you may make more income when you have earned a college degree. Or, you may not. This depends on circumstances such as job availability and pay scale in the chosen industry. Each person must decide which opportunity will be most beneficial.

EXERCISE 20

Name the Opportunity Cost:

1. Planting bush beans in a garden.

    a. Tools that could have been used.
    b. Water that was used.
    c. Other vegetables that could have been planted.
    d. None of these.

2. Staying up late to study for a test.

    a. A good night's sleep.
    b. Energy to complete the test.
    c. Alertness to remember the information.
    d. All of these.

3. Starting a small business.

    a. Benefits and regular income from working for a company.
    b. Access to a soda machine.
    c. Not having a regular paycheck.
    d. All of these.

4. Going to college full-time.

    a. Full-time income lost from working.
    b. Buying books.
    c. Not having to take classes and tests.
    d. None of these.

5. Working full-time instead of going to college.

    a. Less sleep.
    b. College degree to potentially increase income.
    c. Having more time with friends.
    d. None of these.

LESSON 21 - TIME VALUE OF MONEY

The **time value of money** (TVM) states that money available today (**present value or PV**) has more value than the same amount of money in the future (**future value or FV**) due to its earning potential. TVM affects personal, business, and government finance.

When money is invested rather than spent or saved without earning interest, it does not hold the same value in the future. For example, if you have $1,000 and put it in a drawer today and then take it out in ten years, you would still have $1,000. However, if you take the same $1,000 and put it in an interest-bearing account today earning 5% per year, you would have $1,647.01 in ten years. The TVM for the $1,000 in that situation is $647.01. Earning $647.01 in ten years is not all that much, but what if you start with $10,000 and earn 5% for 35 years? You would have $57,337.18. This shows how time increases the value of money.

Invested money earns interest.

When using simple or compound interest to allow money to grow over time, the money is then working by itself. In other words, a person is not doing anything extra to earn additional income. The interest earned over time is called **investment income**.

The difference between simple and compound interest is how the interest is earned. **Simple interest** is earned by calculating it against the principal amount on the loan. For example, the interest rate to be earned or paid is multiplied by the principal amount of the loan and the number of periods in a loan. The formula for calculating simple interest is as follows: principal amount (PV) x interest rate (r) x number of periods (usually years) in the investment or loan (Y).

EXAMPLE 21-1

Suppose: Jennifer invests $15,000 at an interest rate of 6.5% for 10 years. What is the future value of her investment if she earns simple interest?

Answer: $24,750

Interest Earned = 15,000 x .065 x 10
Interest Earned = 9,750
FV= $24,750 (15,000 + 9,750)

To increase the earning potential of a simple interest investment, the investor can make monthly additions to their investment to increase the principal amount. For the purposes of this textbook, we will explore investments without monthly additional deposits; this concept is included in more advanced finance textbooks. While simple interest, in the example above, accrues interest on the principal investment only, **compound interest** accrues on both the principal and the interest earned from previous periods. Investments using compound interest typically have higher earning potential than simple interest investments.

SIMPLE INTEREST VERSUS COMPOUND INTEREST INVESTMENT							
Year	Principal Amount	Periods	Interest Rate	Total Simple Interest Earned	Simple Interest Investment Balance	Compounded Interest Earned Each Period	Compounded Interest Investment Balance
1	15,000	1	6.50%	975.00	15,975.00	975.00	15,975.00
2	15,000	2	6.50%	1,950.00	16,950.00	1038.38	17,013.38
3	15,000	3	6.50%	2,925.00	17,925.00	1105.87	18,119.24
4	15,000	4	6.50%	3,900.00	18,900.00	1177.75	19,297.00
5	15,000	5	6.50%	4,875.00	19,875.00	1254.30	20,551.30
6	15,000	6	6.50%	5,850.00	20,850.00	1335.83	21,887.13
7	15,000	7	6.50%	6,825.00	21,825.00	1422.66	23,309.80
8	15,000	8	6.50%	7,800.00	22,800.00	1515.14	24,824.94
9	15,000	9	6.50%	8,775.00	23,775.00	1613.62	26,438.56
10	15,000	10	6.50%	9,750.00	24,750.00	1718.51	28,157.06

Using the illustration above, a 10-year investment of $15,000 at a compound interest rate of 6.5%, earns the investor $3,407.06 more than an investment using simple interest. The simple interest earned for the same period is added to the original investment of $15,000. The compound interest earned each period (year) is added to the principal amount. This becomes the new principal balance each period (year). Then the interest earned in the next period is based on the principal balance of the previous period. The interest earned is earning money along with the initial deposit of $15,000.

There are several ways to see the effects of compound interest in an investment. The first way is using the "Rule of 72." The Rule of 72 (as shown in the illustration below) is easy to use and it shows how long it will take to double an investment at a particular interest rate. For example, if a person invests $100 at 10%, how long will it take the $100 investment to double? The answer is 7.2 years. To calculate the Rule of 72, a person takes 72 and divides it by the interest rate (as a whole number). Therefore, in the example above when 72 is divided by 10 (representing 10%), the outcome is 7.2 or 7.2 years. Below is an illustration of the Rule of 72 at various interest rates.

RULE OF 72													
72	1.00%	1.50%	2.00%	4.00%	5.00%	6.00%	7.00%	8.00%	9.00%	10.00%	12.00%	16.00%	18.00%
# of Years to Double Investment	72	48	36	18	14.4	12	10.3	9	8	7.2	6	4.5	4

It is also beneficial to look at how an investment will grow over time. What would happen if you put $5,000 into an investment earning 8% when you are 20 years old, then add to that investment each month, and lets it grow until you are 70 years old? How much would the investment grow over time? Example 21-2, on the next page, will answer these questions.

Investments with compound interest increases earning potential!

EXAMPLE 21-2

Suppose: Henry, who is 20 years old, invests $5,000 at an interest rate of 8% for 50 years, compounding monthly. Starting from the beginning of his investment, he contributes $100 each month. What is the future value of his investment when he turns 70 years old?

Answer: The future value of his investment is $1,062,563.66. That is not a typo or a calculation error. Compounding interest helps investments grow at a fast rate, especially if deposits are made toward the investment on a monthly basis.

50-Year Investment Using Compound Interest						
Year	Year Deposits	Monthly Deposit Amount	Year Interest	Total Deposits	Total Interest Earned	Balance
1	1,200.00	100.00	468.29	6,200.00	468.29	6,668.29
5	1,273.68	106.14	1,108.27	11,182.76	3,870.39	15,053.15
10	1,372.08	114.34	2,297.68	17,843.48	12,775.16	30,618.64
15	1,478.16	123.18	4,119.69	25,019.12	29,422.98	54,442.10
20	1,592.40	132.70	6,888.05	32,749.40	57,868.10	90,617.50
25	1,715.40	142.95	11,070.45	41,076.80	104,170.86	145,247.66
30	1,848.00	154.00	17,364.01	50,047.52	177,381.80	227,429.32
35	1,990.80	165.90	26,807.74	59,711.60	291,008.48	350,720.08
40	2,144.64	178.72	40,949.96	70,122.68	465,200.31	535,322.99
45	2,310.36	192.53	62,097.75	81,338.00	730,003.96	811,341.96
50	2,489.04	207.42	93,688.84	93,420.44	1,130,213.59	1,223,634.03

To determine the earning potential of an investment using compound interest you can use an online calculator, calculate by hand using the formula, use Excel, or a financial calculator. Www.Investor.gov/tools/calculators/compound-interest-calculator is a good online calculator.

The formula is $FV = P(1 + r/n)^{Yn}$

FV is the future value
P is the present value or principal
r is the annual interest rate
n equals the number of compounding periods each year
Y is the number of years of the investment.

It is important to note that different investment products use compounding interest at different intervals such as monthly or annually. It is important to know the compounding periods when choosing an investment product.

Let's try using the formula to determine the future value (FV) with the following information: $5,000 present value, 8%, 10 years, and compounding monthly.

$$FV = 5{,}000\ (1 + .08/12)^{10(12)}$$
$$FV = 5{,}000\ (1 + 0.007)^{10(12)}$$
$$FV = 5{,}000\ (1.007)^{10(12)}$$
$$FV = 5{,}000\ (1.007)^{120}$$
$$FV = 11{,}547.99$$

When using the compound interest calculator on the investor.gov website, the answer is $11,098.20 and is more accurate than the answer obtained using a scientific calculator. This is due to rounding issues when dividing the rate by the number of compounding periods. Rounding issues only occur when dividing the rate by the number of compounding terms which can result in an uneven number.

When calculating by hand, a scientific calculator is necessary. These are available as apps or can be purchased. When making the last calculation on a scientific calculator using the 5,000 (1.007)120 in the example, the entry on the calculator would be 5,000 x 1.007 xy 120 (xy is a key on the calculator that must be used).

EXAMPLE 21-3

Suppose: John invests $10,000 at an interest rate of 6% for 15 years compounding annually.

Answer: $23,965.58 - Because the investment is compounded annually, there will not be a rounding issue when using the scientific calculator.

$$FV = 10{,}000\ (1 + .06/1)^{15(1)}$$
$$FV = 10{,}000\ (1 + 0.06)^{15(1)}$$
$$FV = 10{,}000\ (1.06)^{15(1)}$$
$$FV = 10{,}000\ (1.06)^{15}$$
$$FV = 23{,}965.58$$

EXAMPLE 21-4

Suppose: John invests $3,000 at an interest rate of 6% for 35 years compounding monthly.

Answer: $24,370.65

$$FV = 3{,}000\ (1 + .06/12)^{35(12)}$$
$$FV = 3{,}000\ (1 + 0.005)^{35(12)}$$
$$FV = 3{,}000\ (1.005)^{35(12)}$$
$$FV = 3{,}000\ (1.005)^{420}$$
$$FV = 24{,}370.65$$

EXERCISE 21

Multiple Choice Problems:

1. Which of the following best describes the time value of money:
   a. Money available in the future has more value than the same amount of money in that is available to day due to its earning potential.
   b. Money available today has more value than the same amount of money in the future due to its earning potential.
   c. Money available today has less value than the same amount of money in the future due to its earning potential.
   d. None of the above

2. The value of money that a person has today is called:
   a. Present value
   b. Current value
   c. Forthcoming value
   d. Future value

3. The value of money that a person will have in the future is called:
   a. Present value
   b. Current value
   c. Forthcoming value
   d. Future value

4. The Compound Interest formula is:
   a. $PV = P(1 + r/n)^{Yn}$
   b. $PV = FV(1 + r/n)^{Yn}$
   c. $FV = P(1 + r/n)^{Yn}$
   d. $P = FV(1 + r/n)^{Yn}$

5. Sally invests $10,000 at an interest rate of 5.5% for 15 years. What is the future value of her investment if she earns simple interest:
   a. $17,500
   b. $18,250
   c. $15,500
   d. $18,000

The answers to the following questions are based on using a compound interest calculator online at www.investor.gov/tools/calculators/compound-interest-calculator. Explanations and answers using the scientific calculator are in the solutions manual. The two answers will be close in dollar amount.

6. A person invests $4,000 for 25 years at an interest rate of 7% compounded annually. Which answer is the closest to the future value of their investment:
   a. $15,478.74
   b. $21,709.73
   c. $17,167.48
   d. $22,901.67

7. A person invests $4,000 for 25 years at an interest rate of 7% compounded monthly. Which answer is the closest to the future value of their investment:
   a. $15,478.74
   b. $21,709.73
   c. $17,167.48
   d. $22,901.67

8. A person invests $23,000 for 20 years at an interest rate of 5% compounded annually. Which answer is the closest to the future value of their investment:
   a. $61,025.85
   b. $73,764.12
   c. $62,390.73
   d. $76,134.70

9. A person invests $23,000 for 20 years at an interest rate of 5% compounded monthly. Which answer is the closest to the future value of their investment:
   a. $59,025.85
   b. $73.764.12
   c. $63,390.73
   d. $76,134.70

10. A person invests $7,000 for 40 years at an interest rate of 6% compounded monthly. Which answer is the closest to the future value of their investment:
    a. $70,000.03
    b. $76,702.18
    c. $104,821.20
    d. $114,179.88

LESSON 22 - CASH

Bartering was the first form of monetary exchange for goods and services. Doctors were paid with goods in exchange for medical care, people exchanged sugar for flour, a bag of apples for a bag of oranges, and so on. Bartering for goods soon gave way to payment with coins. At later points in time, paper money entered the market, checks were introduced, and finally, payment was made with plastic cards.

When we think of cash, we think of paper money and coins. Cash in the world of finance, banking, and accounting includes money in checking and savings accounts, marketable securities, and government bonds. Checks are also considered a form of cash. All of these items are considered to be cash because each can be converted to cash quickly or within a year. In business, a company's current assets are considered a form of cash.

Today, many people do not use paper money or coins; they conduct most of their transactions with debit cards. Debit cards look like credit cards and can be used as such when making purchases for goods and services such as groceries or department store items. Debit cards can also be used as automatic teller machine (ATM) cards to withdraw and deposit money into checking and savings accounts at ATMs. When a debit card is used for a purchase, it debits the money for the purchase from the checking account to which it is attached. Individuals who have only savings accounts are issued ATM cards which cannot be used as debit cards.

did you KNOW?

Debit cards can be used for puchases and at ATM machines.

It is important to retain all debit card receipts, whether from ATM transactions or purchases, to input into a check register. Receipts are important to keep in case an item needs to be returned or exchanged at the store and to keep track of expenses. A person returning an item could receive back less money than they spent on an item if they do not have their receipt. For example, if you purchased a product for $25 on a Monday and the store put that same product on sale for $20 on Wednesday, the store will only refund $20 if you try to return that product on Wednesday without a receipt. Consumers must show proof of how much they paid for the product they wish to return. Additionally, some companies will only offer store credit, not refunds, for items returned without a receipt.

Interestingly, even with all of the advances in technology, person-to-person and person-to-business bartering still occurs, and cash and checks are still used today. For example, Susie may trade weekly massages for bookkeeping service with a massage therapist. Or, neighbors may exchange fruit and vegetables with other from their gardens and fruit trees. Many small businesses only accept checks or paper money for payment in order to defer costs associated with debit and credit card purchases. Each time a person uses their debit card, the merchant has to pay a transaction fee. Because checks are still necessary today, it is important to learn how to write checks; this will be addressed in the Checking Accounts section of this working textbook.

EXERCISE 22

True or False:

1. True or False. Plastic cards were the first form on money.
2. True or False. Marketable securities are a form of cash.
3. True or False. Checks are considered to be cash.
4. True or False. Debit card receipts for purchases can be thrown away immediately.
5. True or False. It is necessary to know how to write a check in today's society.
6. True or False. Current assets are not considered a form of cash.
7. True or False. An ATM card that is tied to a savings account can be used for purchases.
8. True or False. Debit cards are tied to checking accounts, can be used to make purchases at retail stores, and to withdraw and deposit money in checking and savings accounts at ATMs.
9. True or False. Many small businesses only accept paper money and checks as a form of payment.
10. True or False. Receipts are never necessary for a full refund of a purchase product.

LESSON 23 - DEBT

As discussed in the Liabilities Section, **debt** is money owed. This can be short-term or long-term debt. Debt is a financial tool that must be used wisely.

In today's society, it is almost impossible for adults to avoid debt. Signing an annual lease to rent an apartment creates a short-term debt or liability. Agreeing to a two-year cell phone contract creates a long-term liability. Purchasing a house using a loan incurs a long-term debt or liability.

It is not always a bad thing to have an apartment lease or a mortgage as people need a place to live. The problem with debt arises when an individual's debt load does not fit within their income level. For example, if Joan's net wage for a month is $1,000, and she has an $800 monthly mortgage payment, she will have issues with paying all of her other expenses such as utilities bills, property taxes, house maintenance, groceries, and auto fuel. This situation is called being **house poor**. This can also happen when a lease is so costly it leaves little discretionary income.

Mortgage payments should be modest compared to income.

Additional issues with debt occur when it is used as a source of income such as with credit cards. When monthly expenses, or wants, become greater than net income and credit cards are used to supplement income, consumers can get into financial trouble.

Viewing debt as a tool rather than some elusive, untouchable thing, helps people put their spending into perspective. Asking the question, "How will incurring this debt affect me in the future?" helps when making financial decisions. For example, if taking on more debt now will prevent you from opportunities in the future, then you should avoid that debt.

EXAMPLE 23-1

Suppose: Erin wants to be a culinary expert. After graduating from culinary school, she plans to travel the world to enhance her culinary skills. She plans to make money working at various restaurants in other countries. Between saving up money, working, and assistance from her parents, she will not have any school debt upon graduating. Recently, Erin saw a really nice car and is thinking of getting a loan in order to buy the car. What should she do?

Answer: Avoid the loan. Obtaining a loan for the car will mean a monthly payment which may be difficult to pay if she does not get steady work or make enough money while traveling the world for her culinary experience pursuits. In this situation, the debt of an auto loan could mean Erin will no longer have the opportunity to pursue her culinary dreams. Plus, Erin cannot take the car with her on her world travels.

Example 23-1 illustrates how, sometimes, a loan is not a good use of debt and can thwart opportunities. However, in some situations, debt can be used to open the door to opportunities, as demonstrated in Example 23-2.

EXAMPLE 23-2

Suppose: Zach would like to attend college after graduating high school. He will be 18 years old in April. He realizes he will have to work fulltime to support himself and attend college. He currently makes minimum wage working at a fast food restaurant, which he has discovered will not be enough to live on and pay for college. A friend of his, Mike, graduated high school two years earlier and works as an EMT while attending online college. He has suggested that Zach look into becoming an EMT. The problem is that the EMT courses costs $700 and the exams cost another $300. Zach is able to get a loan for $1,000 to pay for both the course and exams. He will have several options for employment once he completes the EMT schooling. While researching information about becoming an EMT, Zach calculates the average wages for EMTs and discovers he would earn enough to pay for living expenses, college, and pay off the $1,000 loan within a few months of starting work. Would this be a wise use of debt?

Answer: Yes, it would be. Zach would incur $1,000 in debt; however, he currently makes enough money to make the monthly loan payment in addition to his other expenses. Once Zach passes the course and exams, he will begin working fulltime. Also, he will earn a higher wage for his newly acquired skill as an EMT than he currently earns working at fast food restaurants. His increase in pay will allow him to make enough money to quickly pay off the debt.

While avoiding debt can be beneficial in some situations, debt can be used as a tool to open up opportunities for increased income. Learning how to use debt appropriately is important. Many people incur debt without considering what may happen in the future, such as decreased wages or loss of income.

Some people think that incurring debt will increase their chances of becoming rich. In most cases, this simply is not true. You should ask two questions when you consider taking on debt: 1) "What opportunities will be available to me, either now or in the future, if I incur this debt?" and 2) "Do I have sufficient monetary resources to pay back the debt in a timely manner?"

Debt does not create wealth!

While some debt can open up opportunities, as is seen in Example 23-2 or with many college degrees, it rarely leads to increased wealth. In Example 23-2, Zach could just as easily wait to get his EMT license once he saved up enough money to pay for the courses and exams without a loan; however, that is not always feasible.

EXERCISE 23

True or False:

1. True or False. Debt never has to be incurred by anyone.
2. True or False. Incurring debt always leads to wealth.
3. True or False. Debt can sometimes open opportunities.
4. True or False. It is okay to use credit card as a source of cash.
5. True or False. Debt is a financial tool that should be used wisely.

Multiple Choice Problems:

6. Debt is defined as:
    a. Money that is owned.
    b. Money that is owed.
    c. Money that is received as a gift.
    d. Money that is given as a gift.
7. When a person's mortgage payment, property taxes, and utility costs are a large percentage of their total income, it is called:
    a. Debt poor
    b. Mortgage poor
    c. House poor
    d. Always poor
8. Which of the following is true:
    a. Incurring debt will make a person rich.
    b. Incurring debt will make life easier.
    c. Incurring debt is always necessary.
    d. Incurring debt should be used wisely as a financial tool.
9. Which of the following is considered a short-term debt:
    a. A one-year apartment lease.
    b. A two-year cell contract phone contract.
    c. Weekly grocery receipt.
    d. Utility bill.
10. Which of the following is considered long-term debt:
    a. A one-year apartment lease.
    b. A 15-year mortgage.
    c. Money spent at the movies.
    d. A six-month loan.

QUIZ - SECTION 6

True or False:

1. True or False. An opportunity cost is that which is lost when one opportunity is chose over an alternative opportunity.
2. True or False. The time value of money states that money available today has more value than the same amount of money in the future.
3. True or False. Bartering no longer exists.
4. True or False. Debt is money owned.
5. True or False. An opportunity cost can be associated with time.
6. True or False. Interest earned over time is called investment income.
7. True or False. Cash does not include marketable securities.
8. True or False. Debt can be used as a financial tool.
9. True or False. The time value of money affects personal, business, and governmental finance.
10. True or False. It is okay to throw away receipts immediately.

Name the Opportunity Cost:

11. Planting carrots in the garden.
    a. Using tools.
    b. Using water.
    c. Planting other vegetables.
    d. None of these.

12. Staying up late completing a term paper.
    a. Studying for test.
    b. Being alert the next day.
    c. A good night's sleep.
    d. All of these.

13. Starting a personal business.
    a. Sleeping in every day.
    b. Benefits and regular wages from working for a company.
    c. Not having regular income.
    d. None of these.

14. Buying trendy clothes.
    a. Money saved.
    b. Popularity with friends.
    c. Both a and b.
    d. Neither a or b.

Multiple Choice Problems:

15. A person invests $8,000 for 30 years at an interest rate of 8% compounded annually. What is the future value of their investment:
    a. $87,485.84
    b. $80,501.26
    c. $60,898.04
    d. $64,931.98

16. A person invests $9,000 for 30 years at an interest rate of 6% compounded monthly. What is the future value of their investment:
    a. $51,691.42
    b. $46,686.49
    c. $60,898.04
    d. $54,203.18

17. A person invests $2,000 for 20 years at an interest rate of 6% compounded monthly. What is the future value of their investment:
    a. $5,595.42
    b. $6,826.49
    c. $6,620.41
    d. $5,903.36

18. A person invests $15,000 for 40 years at an interest rate of 5% compounded annually. What is the future value of their investment:
    a. $110,376.26
    b. $105,599.83
    c. $113,951.71
    d. $119,528.70

19. Which of the following defines present value:
    a. The value of money today.
    b. The value of money in the future.
    c. Yesterday's value of money.
    d. All of these.

20. What type of account is a debit card attached to:
    a. Savings account
    b. CD account
    c. Checking account
    d. Credit card account

SECTION 7 - CHECKING ACCOUNTS

KEYWORDS

Available balance

Field-of-membership

For-profit

Mutual ownership model

Non-profit

Not-for-profit

Reconciliation

Schedule of fees

LEARNING OBJECTIVES FOR SECTION 7

Upon successful completion of Section 7, you will be able to:

- Differentiate between financial account types.
- Know how to open a checking and savings account.
- Reconcile a checking and savings account.
- Write a check.

LESSON 24 - TYPES OF FINANCIAL INSTITUTIONS

Financial institutions come in many forms including commercial banks, credit unions, savings and loans, investment banks, insurance companies, finance companies, building societies, and asset management companies. This lesson focuses on the first three: commercial banks, credit unions, and savings and loans.

When the word *bank* is mentioned, most people think of commercial banks. Commercial banks have a variety of products for consumers including checking accounts, savings accounts, personal and business loans, and deposit accounts such as IRAs and CDs. Banks are *for-profit* corporations. **For-profit** organizations focus on the goal of a making profit and their operations are designed to achieve this goal. Banks pay their declared earnings to the stockholders/shareholders of the bank. There are no membership qualifications to meet in order to open an account at a bank

Credit unions are much like banks in that they offer the same services and products such as checking accounts, savings accounts, personal and business loans, and deposit accounts to consumers. However, credit unions are not-for-profit corporations. While **not-for-profit** organizations earn profits, these do not go to their owners/members but are put back into the organization to meet their goals. Their declared earnings are paid back to their members through lower fees and loan rates. In order to open accounts with a credit union, a person must become a member and open a savings account, which is called a share account.

Generally, credit unions have **field-of-membership** qualifications that each applicant must meet to become a member. Typical qualifications are based on criteria such as where a person lives, the industry or entity for which they work, or family members who are already members. The field-of-membership qualifications are different at each credit union. Once the applicant meets the field-of-membership qualifications for a particular credit union, they usually have to pay a nominal membership fee. The membership fee is usually returned to the account holder when the account is closed if the account has been in existence for six or more months. If a member closes their account within six months of becoming a member, they typically forfeit their membership fee. Savings accounts are called share accounts because each member has one equal share in the credit union; members are shareholders of their credit union.

Not-for-profit is different from non-profit in that not-for-profit organizations earn revenues through selling products and services and must reinvest a percentage of their annual net profit or declared earnings into the organization. **Non-profit** organizations earn revenues mostly through charitable donations and/or grants and they are limited in how much net profit they can earn each year.

Savings and Loans offer the same services as banks and credit unions and have two types of ownership. They can be owned by depositors and borrowers, known as the mutual ownership model, or they can be owned by shareholders. There are no field-of-membership qualifications for savings and loans that are mutually owned by their members or by shareholders.

EXERCISE 24

Fill in the Blanks.

1. ____________________ ____________________ are not-for-profit organizations.

2. Financial institutions that have two different types of ownership are called ____________________ and ____________________.

3. For-profit financial institutions are called ____________________ ____________________.

4. Credit unions have ____________________ of ____________________ qualifications.

5. Banks pay their declared earnings to ____.

6. A financial institution that has mutual owners, but not field of membership qualifications are called ____________________ ____________________ ____________________.

7. Credit unions pay their declared earnings back to their ____________________ through lower ____________________ and ____________________.

8. For-profit organizations focus on making a ____________________ through ____________________.

9. ____________________ ____________________ ____________________ is where depositors and borrowers own a savings and loan.

10. Companies earn revenues through contributions and/or grants are called ____________________-____________________ organizations.

LESSON 25 - CHECKING ACCOUNTS

While many people have checking accounts, there are many people who do not. According to the Federal Deposit Insurance Corporation (FDIC) in their 2013 FDIC National Survey of Unbanked and Underbanked Households, "7.7 percent (1 in 13) of households in the United States were unbanked in 2013. This proportion represented nearly 9.6 million households." That is a significant number of households. The report does not state if it included those who have accounts with other types of financial institutions such as credit unions.

Having a checking and savings accounts is not mandatory, but these are very useful financial tools. Many people are concerned about losing their money at a bank or credit union; however, unlike the run on the banks in the movie, It's a Wonderful Life, deposits in financial institutions are insured up to certain dollar amounts. The FDIC provides insurance up to $250,000 for each depositor at each insured bank. The National Credit Union Association (NCUA) also provides insurance up to $250,000 for each shareowner (member) for each insured credit union.

In Lesson 24, we noted to open any account at a credit union, a share (savings) account must be opened first. Banks do not have this requirement. However, it is a good idea to open a savings and checking account at the same time if you have no savings accounts at other financial institutions.

Most financial institutions require photo identification, proof of residence, social security number, and date of birth from the applicant to open a new account. A driver's license or a state identification card will usually satisfy the photo identification, proof of residence, and date of birth requirement as long as the current residence matches the address. Financial institutions submit the information to an online verification program. If all of the information matches, the process moves forward. If any of the information, such as social security number or date of birth, do not match, the financial institution will probably request the original document for the item in question, such as a social security card or birth certificate.

This verification process is required by law. Once it is complete, the financial institution obtains a credit report. Most young adults do not have any sort of credit history, and therefore, no credit score. Credit scores are also known as FICO scores. If the applicant does have a credit history, the financial institution will decide if they qualify for a checking account. Most people can open a savings account regardless of their credit history and score.

When you open a checking account for the first time, it is a good idea to have the institution order checks and a debit card. The debit card gives access to the checking and savings account through the ATM when the institution is closed. It is important to note that financial institutions charge fees when you use a foreign (ATM not owned by the financial institution where the account is held) ATM. Both the financial institution and the institution where the ATM is used will charge a transaction fee of $1 to $5. Debit cards can also be used for purchases at most merchants; however, there are still companies that do not accept debit cards. Checks are necessary if the purchaser does not have cash and if the merchant does not accept debit cards. The problem with checks is that many people do not know how to complete one. Let's learn how right now!

Another important aspect of a checking account is the associated fees. Every financial institution has a schedule of fees, and it is important to compare fees before selecting a financial institution. Fees that may be incurred with a financial institution include the use of the checking account, going below the required minimum balance, per check used, and foreign ATM fees. Check with the institution and ask for a copy of their schedule of fees or look for a list of fees on their website.

In a checking account, the account balance does not always match the available balance. This is due to the timing of when a merchant puts a hold on funds and when they push through a batch of transactions for the day. For example, John has a checking account balance of $500. He purchases a fishing rod from the store, GO Fishing, at 10:00 a.m. for $50 using his debit card. When he looks at his account at 2:00 p.m., it states he has an account balance of $500 and an available balance of $450. GO Fishing put a hold on the $50 purchase, but they will not run their batch of transactions through their system until later that night, or possibly until the next day. Once GO Fishing runs their batch of transactions through their financial institution, and John does not make any more purchases, his account balance and available balance will match. The illustration below is a sample blank check:

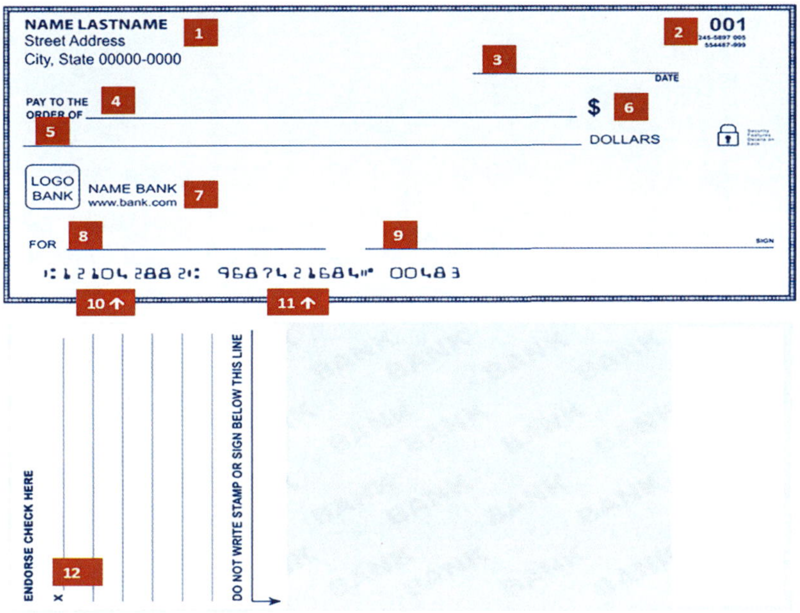

1. Name and address of the account holder(s).

2. Number of the check. Checks are printed in sequential numerical order.

3. Date check is written.

4. Name of payee (e.g. person or company being paid).

5. Dollar amount being paid written in words.

6. Dollar amount being paid written in numeric form.

7. Name of the financial institution where the account is held.

8. Optional field to state the purpose of the check (i.e. shoes for work).

9. Signature of the account holder.

10. Routing number of the financial institution where the account is held.

11. Account number of the checking account that funds are drawn on.

12. The payee of the check endorses (sign) the back of the check to either deposit or cash the check. When cashing a check, the payee obtains the amount being paid in cash.

The following illustration is an example of a complete check.

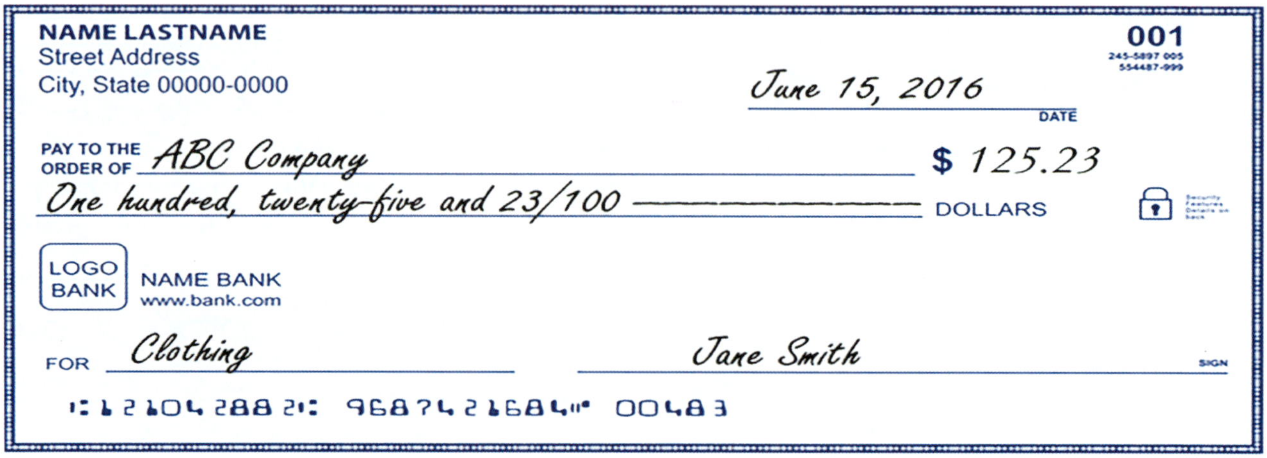

The written dollar amount is to be formatted in a particular way. The dollar part is written out while the cents are written as a fraction. It is always written with the cents on top and *100* written on the bottom as shown in the illustration. Compound numbers, such as the *25* in the illustration, are always hyphenated.

Examples of written numbers for checks are as follows:

- $5.73 – Five and 73/100 ----------
- $11.67 – Eleven and 67/100 ----------
- $463.78 – Four hundred, sixty-three and 78/100 ----------
- $1,689.45 – One thousand, six hundred, eighty-nine and 45/100 ----------
- $23,953.84 – Twenty-three thousand, nine hundred, fifty-three and 84/100 ----------
- $487,279.30 – Four hundred, eighty-seven thousand, two hundred, seventy-nine and 30/100 ---

Another important aspect of a checking account is the associated fees. Every financial institution has a **schedule of fees**, and it is important to compare fees before selecting a financial institution. Fees that may be incurred with a financial institution include the use of the checking account, going below the required minimum balance, per check used, and foreign ATM fees. Check with the institution and ask for a copy of their schedule of fees or look for a list of fees on their website.

All financial institutions have fees!

In a checking account, the account balance does not always match the **available balance**. This is due to the timing of when a merchant puts a hold on funds and when they push through a batch of transactions for the day. For example, John has a checking account balance of $500. He purchases a fishing rod from the store, GO Fishing, at 10:00 a.m. for $50 using his debit card. When he looks at his account at 2:00 p.m., it states he has an account balance of $500 and an available balance of $450. GO Fishing put a hold on the $50 purchase, but they will not run their batch of transactions through their system until later that night, or possibly until the next day. Once GO Fishing runs their batch of transactions through their financial institution, and John does not make any more purchases, his account balance and available balance will match.

EXERCISE 25

For questions 1 – 6, fill out the following check with the following information:

Jessica Smith purchased a swimsuit for a vacation trip for $38.56 from Swimsuits R Us on May 11, 2013.

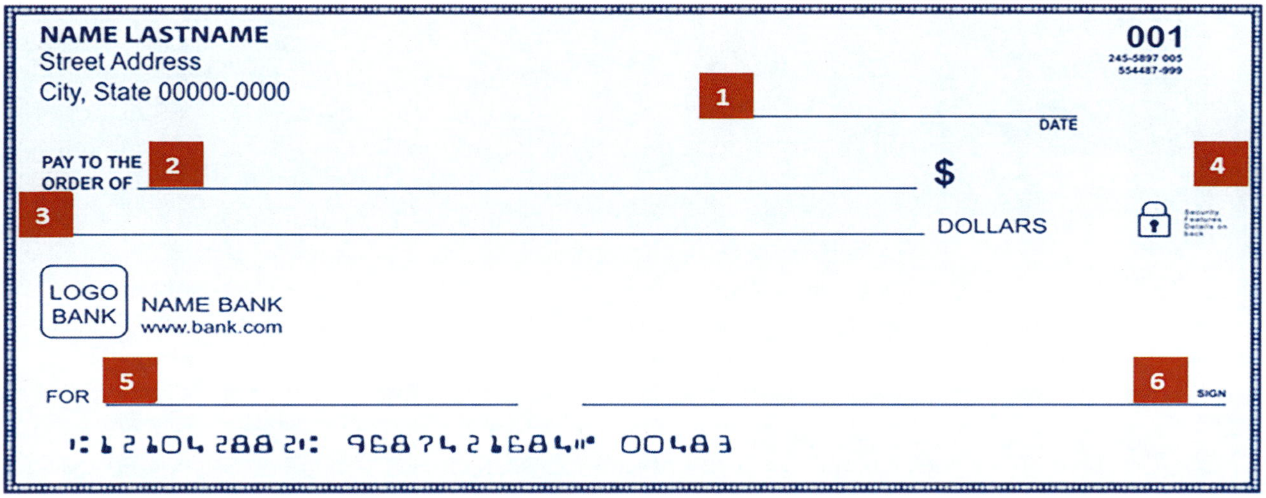

7. $386.46 would be written as follows:
    a. Three hundred, eightsix and 46/100 ------
    b. Three hundred and eighty-six and 46/100 -------
    c. Three hundred, eighty-six and 46/100 -------
    d. Three hundred, eight-six and forty-six/100 ------

8. Financial institution charge various fees for their checking accounts using
    a. a Schedule of Fees
    b. a Schedule of Accounts
    c. a Schedule of Charges
    d. None of these.

9. Money in accounts in banks and credit unions are insured
    a. up to $300,000 for each depositor even if the institution is not insured.
    b. up to $300,000 for each depositor per insured institution.
    c. up to $250,000 for each depositor even if the institution is not insured.
    d. up to $250,000 for each depositor per insured institution.

10. Each checking account has an account balance and a(n)
    a. accessible balance
    b. manageable balance
    c. available balance
    d. convenient balance

LESSON 26 - SAVINGS ACCOUNTS

The process of opening a savings account is relatively the same as opening a checking account, except the institution does not usually run a credit report. Every savings/share account and checking account has its own unique account number.

Using a savings account can help unexpected expenses.

Savings accounts typically do not have a difference between the account balance and the available balance because funds are deposited or withdrawn immediately rather than by using a debit card for purchases or writing checks. The exception to this is with credit unions. The membership amount that was required at the time of opening a share account is not available for use by the account holder. For example, if ABC Credit Union requires $25 to open a share account, that $25 is shown in the account balance, but because the $25 is part of the membership, it is not available for use. The $25 is usually returned to the account holder when the account is closed. Once a person opens a share account with a credit union, they can open other accounts without any other required deposit amount.

Banks, on the other hand, do not have memberships and do not require membership deposit amounts. However, many banks require a minimum deposit amount for some savings account products. Many banks have monthly fees for checking accounts; however, many banks will waive the monthly fee if the account holder sets up an automatic deposit into a savings account each month and maintains a minimum balance. This encourages the account holder to save money.

The insured amount by the FDIC and NCUA also applies to savings accounts. The insured amount of $250,000 covers each depositor. Therefore, a married couple could have up to $500,000 insured, $250,000 each, in one account at an insured institution.

If an applicant does not qualify for a checking account due to a low credit score and poor credit history, opening a savings account is the next best step. Financial institutions will work with those who have poor credit histories in order to assist them in working toward opening a checking account in the future. Many financial institutions will require a savings account to be in good standing for a period of time, such as six months. They may also require the new account holder to meet other goals, such as improving their credit history with no new debt, paying down debt, and/or improving their FICO score by a certain amount or percentage.

If an applicant has to wait to open a checking account, they will need to manage their money using their savings account. One disadvantage of using a savings account, as stated in Lesson 3, is the minimum withdrawal limits for savings accounts set by Federal law. A savings account is permitted six withdrawals per month. Those withdrawals include outgoing transfers. Once a depositor has reached six withdrawals or outgoing transfers in a given month, a fee for any successive withdrawals will be charged by the financial institution. Each institution charges a different amount.

EXERCISE 26

True or False:

1. True or False. Savings usually don't have a different between the account balance and available balance.

2. True or False. A person can never open a savings account if they have a low FICO score.

3. True or False. The law has a minimum withdrawal limit for savings accounts.

4. True or False. The FDIC is the agency that insures deposits for banks.

5. True or False. The FDIC is the agency that insures deposits for credit unions.

6. True or False. Opening a savings account is relatively the same process as opening a checking account.

7. True or False. The insurable about for each deposit with an insured institution is $275,000.

8. True or False. If a person doesn't qualify for a checking account they can work toward getting a checking account by doing a good job maintaining a savings account.

9. True or False. Banks require a membership in order to open any accounts.

10. True or False. The minimum withdrawal amount for savings account is six per month.

LESSON 27 - MANAGING YOUR ACCOUNTS ~ RECONCILIATION PART I

Reconciling checking accounts each month is extremely important. Not doing so can result in shortages in the account and result in an accumulation of fees for insufficient funds; these can add up quickly. **Reconciliation** of a checking account refers to making adjustments of the differences between a Statement of Account balance and an account holder's balance in their checkbook register. A checkbook register is used to keep track of the debits and credits in an account. A register is also used for savings accounts. To reconcile an account, the account holder matches the debits and credits on the Statement of Account to their checkbook records. Various tools are used to record the debit and credit transactions in a checking account including a paper checkbook register booklet, Excel spreadsheet, and Quicken accounting software. The format may be slightly different in various checkbook registers.

Below is an illustration of a checkbook register.

1	2	3	4	5		6	7
DATE	REF	DESCRIPTION OF TRANSACTION	PAYMENT / DEBIT (-)	R	c	DEPOSIT / CREDIT (+)	BALANCE

1. The date is the date of the transaction or the date on a check.

2. The TYPE is for the type of transaction: enter the check number for a check, DEP for a deposit, WD for a withdrawal, DEBIT when a debit card is used for a transaction, or EFT for payments automatically withdrawn from the account.

3. Description of transaction is the name of the Payee and what was purchased or paid.

4. Payment/Debit (-) is the amount debited or paid. This would include any fees assessed on the account and posted to the account by the financial institution.

5. R and c stand for "reconciled" and "cleared". The c box next to the transaction is checked when an item has gone through checking account at the financial institution. This can be seen by logging into the checking account online or using an app. The R box next the transaction is checked once the checking account has been reconciled.

6. Deposit/Credit (+) is the amount deposited or credited to an account. This would include any interest earned on the account and posted to the account by the financial institution.

7. Balance is the remaining or available balance in the account once all transactions have been entered into the register.

The following illustration shows what a checkbook register looks like when transactions have been entered into it. The following is a list of transactions that have occurred for this example.

- Beginning balance of 150.00 on August 10, 2014.
- Check number 236 written on August 12, 2014, for $8.56 at Arby's.
- Direct deposit of $536.29 paycheck on August 15, 2014.
- ATM withdrawal of $20 on August 16, 2014, to go to the movies.

DATE	REF	DESCRIPTION OF TRANSACTION	PAYMENT / DEBIT (-)	R	c	DEPOSIT / CREDIT (+)	BALANCE
8/10/14		Beginning Balance					150.00
8/12/14	236	Arby's Dining	8.56				141.44
8/15/14	DEP	Paycheck				536.29	677.73
8/16/14	WD	Cash Withdrawal	20.00				657.73

As can be seen in this illustration, the balance reflects the running total of debits and credits being subtracted from or added to the balance. Once you check your checking account online or through an app and see the funds have been cleared or have been released by the financial institution, you would put a check mark in the c box. The next illustration shows the first two items being cleared.

DATE	REF	DESCRIPTION OF TRANSACTION	PAYMENT / DEBIT (-)	R	c	DEPOSIT / CREDIT (+)	BALANCE
8/10/14		Beginning Balance			✓		150.00
8/12/14	236	Arby's Dining	8.56		✓		141.44
8/15/14	DEP	Paycheck				536.29	677.73
8/16/14	WD	Cash Withdrawal	20.00				657.73

Reconcile all accounts every month!

EXERCISE 27

Complete problems 1 – 10 below using the following scenario:
Samantha made the following transactions. Help her out by entering them into the checkbook register.

1. Beginning balance of $200.00 on October 1, 2013.
2. Purchase of groceries for $86.46 at Walmart on October 3, 2013, using a debit card.
3. Check #461 used to pay the water bill to Municipal Water Company for $43.98 on October 2013.
4. Used debit card on October 8, 2013, at Qdoba to eat lunch with friends. Spent $10.43.
5. Cash withdrawal at an ATM on October 12, 2013, for $20 to have on hand.
6. Direct deposit of paycheck for $764.26 on October 15, 2013.
7. Rent of $400 was paid to Lakewood Apartments on October 15, 2013, using check number 462.
8. Samantha checked her account online on October 17, 2013, and saw that all of the transactions cleared her account except check 462. Mark those items as cleared.
9. Samantha uses her debit card to purchase gas at the Flying J for her car on August 18, 2013, for $29.13.
10. On August 20, 2013, Samantha purchases clothes for work at J.C. Penney for $26.46 using her debit card.

DATE	REF	DESCRIPTION OF TRANSACTION	PAYMENT / DEBIT (-)	R	c	DEPOSIT / CREDIT (+)	BALANCE

LESSON 28 - MANAGING YOUR ACCOUNTS ~ RECONCILIATION PART II

At the end of every month, a financial institution either mails a Statement of Account to the account holder or makes it available online at the institution's website. Each financial institution's Statement of Account is formatted differently. On the next page, there is an illustration of an abbreviated Statement of Account by a financial institution.

Below is a checkbook register for the same account represented in the Statement of Account on the next page. Compare the Statement of Account against the checkbook register below. Are there any problems? Is there anything missing or entered incorrectly?

DATE	REF	DESCRIPTION OF TRANSACTION	PAYMENT / DEBIT (-)	R	c	DEPOSIT / CREDIT (+)	BALANCE
		Beginning Balance					1,248.76
4/1/14	DEP	Paycheck				648.79	1,897.55
4/1/14	DEBIT	McDonald's Dining	12.87				1,884.68
4/3/14	DEBIT	Walmart Groceries	156.00				1,728.68
4/10/14	355	Stylist Salon Entertainment	39.46				1,689.22
4/12/14	WD	Withdrawal Reimbursement for Mark	40.00				1,649.22
4/15/14	WD	Apartment Company Rent	400.00				1,249.22
4/15/14	DEP	Paycheck				648.79	1,898.01

When comparing the above checkbook register against the Statement of Account, the discrepancies noted are the Walmart entry of 156.00 and the missing entry of 32.75 for the Flying J. The Walmart entry should be 156.48.

If these had been the actual checkbook register and Statement of Account, the account holder would have discovered the errors and made the corrections in the checkbook register. If a paper register is used to record transactions, an adjusting entry of 33.23 (32.75 – Flying J + 0.48 Walmart error) would be entered and subtracted from the balance. This is done because it would be difficult to erase all of the transactions and reenter them.

If a software program is being used to record transactions, missing transactions can be added to the register and transactions with errors can be corrected.

Now, let's practice with Exercise 28.

Managing your checking account helps prevent over-withdrawing!

STATEMENT OF ACCOUNT ILLUSTRATION

Financial Institution Name
Street Address
City State Zip

Statement of Account
List of Branches
and Phone Numbers

ACCOUNT NUMBER	STATEMENT ENDING DATE	BRANCH	PAGE
0001234567	4/30/2014	26	1 OF 2

Account Holder's Name
Street Address
City State Zip

DATE	TRANSACTION DESCRIPTION			AMOUNT	BALANCE
	01-01-14 THRU 04-30-14		PREVIOUS BALANCE		1,248.76
APR01	DIRECT DEPOSIT	0000123456	XYZ COMPANY	648.79	1,897.55
APR01	DEBIT CARD DEBIT	0000234567	MCDONALDS	12.87	1,884.68
APR03	DEBIT CARD DEBIT	0000345678	WALMART	156.48	1,728.20
APR06	DEBIT CARD DEBIT	0000456789	FLYING J	32.75	1,695.45
APR10	CHECK #355			39.46	1,655.99
APR12	ATM WITHDRAWAL			40.00	1,615.99
APR15	EFT	0000567890	APARTMENT COMPANY	400.00	1,215.99
APR15	DIRECT DEPOSIT	0000123456	XYZ COMPANY	648.79	1,864.78

EXERCISE 28

Below is the checkbook register and the transaction portion of Statement of Account for the same checking account. There are three errors. Can you find them?

CHECKBOOK REGISTER

DATE	REF	DESCRIPTION OF TRANSACTION	PAYMENT / DEBIT (-)	R	c	DEPOSIT / CREDIT (+)	BALANCE
		Beginning Balance					1,114.13
12/1/12	DEP	Paycheck				761.46	1,875.59
12/1/12	946	Heritage Apartments Rent	350.00				1,525.59
12/6/12	DEBIT	Walmart Groceries	97.37				1,428.22
12/12/12	DEBIT	Phillips 66 Fuel or Gas	26.73				1,401.49
12/15/12	DEP	Paycheck Reimbursement for Mark				761.46	2,162.95
12/20/12	WD	Cash Withdrawal Rent	40.00				2,122.95
12/23/12	943	Power Company Electric Bill	95.27				2,027.68
12/27/12	DEBIT	Shoe Carnival Clothing or shoes	35.84				1,991.84
1/1/13	DEBIT	Taco Bell Dining	8.29				1,983.55

STATEMENT OF ACCOUNT

DATE	TRANSACTION DESCRIPTION			AMOUNT	BALANCE
	12-01-12 THRU 12-31-12		PREVIOUS BALANCE		1,114.13
DEC01	DIRECT DEPOSIT	0000123456	DGH COMPANY	761.46	1,875.59
DEC01	CHECK #946			350.00	1,525.59
DEC06	DEBIT CARD DEBIT	000345678	WALMART	98.37	1,427.22
DEC12	DEBIT CARD DEBIT	0000456789	PHILLIPS 66	26.73	1,400.49
DEC15	DIRECT DEPOSIT	0000123456	DGH COMPANY	761.46	2,161.95
DEC20	ATM WITHDRAWAL			40.00	2,121.95
DEC23	CHECK #947			95.27	2,026.68
DEC27	DEBIT CARD DEBIT	0000234567	MOVIE THEATER	22.91	2,003.77
DEC31	DEBIT CARD DEBIT	0000567891	SHOE CARNIVAL	35.84	1,967.93

The three errors are:

1. ______________________________

2. ______________________________

3. ______________________________

QUIZ - SECTION 7

Complete problems 1 – 10 below using the following scenario:
Josh made the following transactions. Help he out by entering them into the checkbook register.

1. Beginning balance of $300.00 on June20, 2015.

2. Direct deposit of paycheck for $1,263.89 on July 1, 2015.

3. Rent of $600 was paid to Westlake Apartments on July 1, 2015, using check number 724.

4. Purchase of groceries for $136.45 at Safeway on July 3, 2015, using a debit card.

5. Cash withdrawal at an ATM on July 4, 2015, for $40 to celebrate 4th of July with family and friends.

6. Josh received a check from his friend, Mark, for $50 on July 11, 2015, reimbursing him for money borrowed.

7. Check #724 used to pay the cell phone bill to Verizon for $60.53 on July 15, 2015.

8. Josh used his debit card to purchase gas at the Conoco for his car on July 15, 2015, for $35.46.

9. On July 17, 2015, Josh has lunch with friends at McDonald's for $9.27 using his debit card.

10. Josh checked his account online on July 15, 2013, and saw that transactions 1 through 5 cleared his account. Mark those transactions as cleared.

	DATE	REF	DESCRIPTION OF TRANSACTION	PAYMENT / DEBIT (-)	R	c (10->)	DEPOSIT / CREDIT (+)	BALANCE
1								
2								
3								
4								
5								
6								
7								
8								
9								

Multiple Choice Problems:

11. A company that earns revenues through selling products and services and reinvests their earned revenues back into the company to benefit its members is known as:
    a. a for-profit company.
    b. a not-for-profit company.
    c. a non-profit company.
    d. a profit company.

12. A company whose focus is making sure their operations make a profit is known as:
    a. a for-profit company.
    b. a not-for-profit company.
    c. a non-profit company.
    d. a profit company.

13. A company who revenues are solely earned through charitable donations and/or grants is known as:
    a. a for-profit company.
    b. a not-for-profit company.
    c. a non-profit company.
    d. a profit company.

14. The two companies that insured the funds deposited at banks and credit unions are the:
    a. FDIC and the NCUA
    b. NDIC and the FCUA
    c. FDUA and the NCIC
    d. FDIA and the NCUC

15. What is the Federal withdrawal limit for savings accounts:
    a. Two withdrawals per month.
    b. Four withdrawals per month.
    c. Six withdrawals per month.
    d. There are no Federal withdrawals limits for savings accounts.

16. Transactions should be recorded into a register:
    a. It doesn't matter when
    b. Immediately
    c. Never
    d. Once a week

17. Reconciling an account should be completed on a ________________ basis:
    a. Quarterly
    b. Weekly
    c. Monthly
    d. Annual

18. ATM cards tied to savings account can be:
    a. Used to make purchases at stores.
    b. Only used to make withdrawals and deposits at ATMs.
    c. Both a and b
    d. None of these

19. $1,683.47 should be written in long-form as follows on a check:
    a. One thousand, six hundred, eighty-three and forty-seven/100 -------
    b. One thousand, six hundred, eightythree and 47/100 -------------------
    c. One thousand, six-hundred, eighty-three and 47/100 ------------------
    d. One thousand, six hundred, eighty-three and 47/100 ------------------

20. When recording a deposit, the following should be written in the type column:
    a. DEP
    b. DEPOSIT
    c. DEBIT
    d. CREDIT

21. Which of the following describes reconciliation of a checking account?
    a. Entering each transaction twice into a checkbook register.
    b. Read the Statement of Account, but not making any corrections.
    c. Not making adjustments of the differences between a Statement of Account balance and an account holder's balance in their checkbook register
    d. Making adjustments of the differences between a Statement of Account balance and an account holder's balance in their checkbook register

22. A payee is:
    a. The financial institution making a payment.
    b. The person making a payment.
    c. The person or company being paid.
    d. All of these are examples of a payee.

23. "R" on a checkbook register stands for:
    a. Recommended
    b. Reconciled
    c. Resolved
    d. There are no Federal transaction limits for checking accounts.

24. What does "cleared" mean when referring to checking accounts?
    a. It is when the financial institution has approved a deposit or payment on an account.
    b. It is when the financial institution has denied a deposit or payment on an account.
    c. It is when the financial institution has cleared an account of all funds.
    d. It is when an account holder has withdrawn all funds from an account.

25. What is the Federal transaction limit for all checking accounts before fees are incurred.
    a. Two transactions per month.
    b. Three transactions per month.
    c. Six transactions per month.
    d. There are no Federal transaction limits for checking accounts.

SECTION 8 - INVESTMENTS

KEYWORDS

Bond rating agencies	Bond rating system
Bond yield	Bonds
Call option	Capital
Capital appreciation	Capital gain
Common stocks	Debtholder
Dividends	Diversification
Equity funds	Fixed-income funds
Fixed interest rate	Investors
Liquidates	Mailbox money
Money manager	Money market funds
Mutual fund	Non-passive income
Over-the-counter	Passive income
Preferred stocks	Put option
Rating system	Risk adverse
Securities	Shareholders
Stock option	Variable interest rate

LEARNING OBJECTIVES FOR SECTION 8

Upon successful completion of Section 8, you will be able to:

- Explain types of investment tools.
- Differentiate between stocks, bonds, mutual funds, and other investments.

LESSON 29 - STOCKS

Securities are investment instruments purchased and sold in the financial market in order to make money for the investors who buy and sell them. Investors put money into a product or service in hopes they will receive greater money in return than the initial investment made. Types of securities are stocks; corporate, municipal, and government bonds; mutual funds; and stock and futures options. Stocks represent ownership in a company. Companies sell stocks to **shareholders**, who are a type of investor who holds shares, or some ownership, in the company from which the stocks are purchased. Companies sell stocks in order to raise money to operate their businesses. The two main categories of stocks are common and preferred.

Companies that liquidate usually sell all of their assets.

Owners of **common stocks** have ownership and voting rights in a company. They get to vote for those who are on the board of directors and on company policy issues. However, they are the last to be paid when a company **liquidates**, or sells all of its assets. Owners of **preferred stocks** have ownership in a company, but they do not usually have any voting rights. On the other hand, if a company liquidates, owners of preferred stock are paid before the investors who own common stocks in the same company. Preferred stock owners also receive dividends before owners of common stocks.

When an investor has the right to buy (known as a **call option**) or sell (known as a **put option**) a stock for a set price for a stated period of time, they have a **stock option**. If the investor does not buy or sell the stock within the allocated time period, the option expires.

In Lesson 3 we discussed **dividends** which are funds paid to shareholders of a company. Dividends are typically paid from the profits of a company. The board of directors of a company decides when dividends are paid to shareholders and how much shareholders will receive. The board of directors can also decide to give different classes of stocks (e.g. common and preferred) different dividend amounts, usually calculated as a percentage of the profits.

Investors purchase stock in order to receive a positive return on their investment. This happens when the company pays dividends. Positive returns also occur when there is **capital appreciation**, or when an investor sells a stock for a higher price than he or she purchased it for. The difference in the higher sale price and the lower purchase price represents the return to the investor. But beware! Stock prices can also go down in value.

Stocks are sold in the securities market. The United States has its own securities markets, and the three largest are the New York Stock Exchange (NYSE), National Association of Securities Dealers Automated Quotation System (Nasdaq), and American Stock Exchange (AMEX). Examples of commodities exchanges are the New York Mercantile Exchange, Inc., (NYMEX), Chicago Board of Trade (CBOT), and London Commodity Exchange (LCE). Commodities exchanges trade contracts in agricultural and mineral products such as wheat, corn, cattle, pigs, gold, and silver.

EXERCISE 29

Across*

1. Acronym for the New York Stock Exchange.
3. A person has this when they have a right to buy a stock.
4. A type of stock where the shareholder usually does not have voting rights.
5. A person has this when they have a right to sell a stock.
6. A type of stock where the shareholder has voting rights.
8. The money paid from profits to shareholders.

Down*

2. When a person has the right to buy or sell a stock for a set period of time and at a set price.
7. When a company goes out of business and sells all of their assets.
9. Instruments that are purchased by investors.
10. Those that own stocks in a company.
11. Those who pay for securities in order to get a higher return than what they invested.

**Answers 7, 8, 9, 10, and 11 are plural.*

LESSON 30 - BONDS

As mentioned in Lesson 29, **bonds** are a type of marketable security. A bond is a debt instrument used by companies and governments. There are corporate, municipal, and government bonds. A bond represents a debt the issuer of the bond owes to the owner of the bond. Bonds are issued by corporations, governments, and other entities, such as states or cities, for an agreed upon period of time. These entities may issue bonds to fund their operations or finance an expansion. The investor purchases the bond, which can earn either a variable or a fixed interest rate. The owner of the bond is called a **debtholder** or creditor.

With most corporate bonds, investors will purchase the bond and will then receive interest payments, called a coupon, usually semi-annually until the maturity date of the bond. At that time, the investor will receive their principal back as well as the final interest payment. Another type of bond is a zero-coupon bond. With this bond the investor purchases the bond at a discounted value from its face amount. Interest builds up over the life of the bond until maturity. At that time the value of a bond is equal to its face amount. For example, a zero-coupon bond has a value of $100 and a five-year maturity date. The investor purchases the bond for $50 and cashes it in for $100 when it matures in five years. The investor's yield on the bond is $50. Government savings bonds are a form of zero-coupon bonds.

Variable interest rates vary over the life of a loan!

A **variable interest rate** can change over the period of the loan; a fixed interest rate stays exactly the same for the entire loan period. A loan can have a combination of a variable and fixed interest rate. For example, a loan can have a fixed interest rate for the first 36 months and then switch to a variable interest rate. Variable interest rates are tied to an index such as U.S. Treasuries.

Just like stocks, corporate and government bonds are traded on the stock exchanges and some are traded **over-the-counter** (OTC). OTC simply means the bond is traded using a tool other than one of the stock exchanges. The major stock exchanges have a list of requirements a security must meet in order to be traded. For smaller companies, their stocks and bonds usually do not meet the list of requirements, so they trade their marketable securities over-the-counter.

Bond rating systems resembling a grading system. Standard & Poor's (S&P), Moody's, and Fitch are the three most respected **bond rating agencies**. Each agency has its own rating system; each system has its own criteria. The ratings gauge a company's ability to pay back their debts. Rating systems differentiate between long-term and short-term debt. Their top rating is a strong indicator that a company can repay their debts, while their bottom rating suggests the company already has debts in default. Each agency has a significant number of ratings in their rating system. You can learn more about each agency's rating system by visiting their website.

A **bond yield** is the difference between what the investor paid for a bond and how much they receive at maturity. The different types of bond yields are yield to maturity (YTM), yield to call (YTC), current yield, realized yield, and nominal yield. The study of these bond yields is outside the scope of this working textbook. It is important to note, though, that there are many different kinds of bonds with a variety of yields.

A bond's par value is the value on the face of the bond. A $1,000 bond will have a par value of $1,000. Bonds are sold into the market priced at par, premium (a value over par) or discount (a value under par). The premium or discount is determined upon the value the bond investor is willing to pay for the bond. This is based partially on the going interest rate available in the market for other investments with similar risk and also the perceived risk of the borrowing entity on the bond. For example, Company Highrate issues bonds at a face rate of 7%. At the time of the issuance, the going interest rate for other bonds with similar risk is at 8%. In order for Highrate to sell their bonds, they would have to sell the bond below the face value so the investor would earn an effective rate of 8%.

If you buy a $1,000 par bond at 7% annual interest, the interest earned each year would be $70 ($1,000 x .07 = $70). If rates increase to 8% for bonds with similar risk, you the investor would want an 8% return on your money, but the interest payment on the bond would remain at $70 per year. The market value of the bond you purchased would be $875 ($70 / .08 (8%) = $875). The bond would have to be sold at a discount of $125 from the $1,000 par value in order to earn the 8% market rate. If rates decrease to 5%, the bond would still earn $70. The market value of the bond would be $1,400 ($70 / .05 = $1,400). The bond would have a premium of $400 over the par value because the interest earned on the bond is at a higher interest rate than what bonds with similar risk are selling for in the market.

EXERCISE 30

Multiple Choice Problems:

1. A fixed interest rate:
    a. stays the same, but changes 90 days into a loan period.
    b. stays the same for the entire loan period.
    c. stays the same for 30 days, but changes each month.
    d. varies according to the index it is tied to.

2. Bonds are a:
    a. type of marketable security.
    b. constraints on a checking account.
    c. something investors should avoid.
    d. None of the above.

3. The three most respected bond rating agencies are:
    a. Standard & Moody's, Poor's, and Fitch
    b. Standard & Poor's, Moody's, and Fitch
    c. Standard & Poor's, Moody's, and Finch
    d. Standard & Fitch, Poor's, and Moody's

4. A variable interest rate:
    a. only varies the last 60 days of a loan.
    b. stays the same for the entire loan period.
    c. varies according to the index it is tied to.
    d. varies according to what the investor wants each month.

5. Over-the-counter bonds:
    a. are traded at the counter at a pharmacy.
    b. are traded at counters in the grocery stores.
    c. use the major stock exchanges.
    d. don't use the major stock exchanges.

6. The owner of a bond is called a:
    a. debtholder.
    b. bond holder.
    c. credit holder.
    d. bond issuer.

7. A bond rating:
    a. measures how much investors like a particular bond issuer.
    b. measures how much investors like a particular bond.
    c. measures the ability that bond issuers can repay their debts.
    d. measures the ability of how much an investor can invest.

8. Each bond rating agency:
    a. has the exact same rating system.
    b. has their own rating system.
    c. guesses what their ratings should be for each bond.
    d. None of the above.

9. Bond yield:
    a. doesn't exist when purchasing bonds.
    b. is the difference between how much an investor paid for a bond and how much the company receives from the same bond.
    c. is the difference between how much a company issued on a bond and how much they receive at from an investor for the bond.
    d. is the difference between how much an investor paid for a bond and how much they receive at maturity.

10. Bonds are:
    a. either corporate or municipal bonds.
    b. either corporate or government bonds.
    c. either corporate, municipal, or government bonds.
    d. either municipal and government bonds.

LESSON 31 - MUTUAL FUNDS

Another marketable security, a **mutual fund**, is comprised of a group of stocks, bonds, and other securities. When an investor purchases a mutual fund, they receive interest in a portion of all the various securities held by that fund. This helps obtain **diversification**; the investor reduces risk by spreading their money over multiple investments rather than depending on one particular stock to perform well. Each shareholder's ownership percentage in the mutual fund is based on how many shares he or she owns, or how much money they have invested. Mutual funds are managed by an investment firm or bank, called a **money manager**. The job of a money manager is to take the capital of a mutual fund and invest it to make more money. **Capital** is the money you or a company has invested to generate income.

A mutual fund pays dividends from the stocks and interest from the bonds held by the fund. As a shareholder, you can wait until a mutual fund increases in price and then sell the fund in order to make a profit. The fund will sometimes sell some of the securities it is comprised of when there has been an increase in price. When the fund sells any of the securities that increased in price, the fund has incurred a capital gain. The capital gain is passed to the investors who then have to pay taxes on it. A **capital gain** is the increase in a capital asset. Investors do not realize the gain until the capital asset is sold. Taxes are incurred when the capital gain is realized.

The three main types of mutual funds are fixed-income funds, money market funds, and equity funds. **Fixed-income funds** are comprised of corporate, municipal, and federal bonds. **Equity funds** invest in both U.S. and global stocks. **Money market funds** are typically comprised of short-term debt securities. One type of short-term (less than one year) debt security is government treasury bills (T-bills). Some funds are targeted to just one particular type of investment. An example is a mutual fund that invests in loans on high-grade commercial office space.

The idea behind mutual funds is to allow investors who do not have enough money to invest in a variety of securities to diversify their investments. Sometimes there are higher costs associated with mutual funds due to fees charged by the mutual fund managers. Some have fees, or a load, paid to the money manager. Some funds are no-load funds but these may assess trading fees to get out of the fund. A fund's performance should always be examined after any fees are taken out. Some companies monitor the performance of mutual funds. This allows investors to judge the performance of various funds to determine which one they want to purchase.

Many investors use online trading companies that offer lower trading costs. Several sites, such as Investopedia, have free virtual trading simulators allowing participants to practice trading with virtual (play) money.

There is no age limit for using Investopedia's Stock Simulator*; however, a person must be 18 years of age or older to invest real money in the securities market. Those younger than 18 years can invest in securities with an adult as the account holder.

**There are public games on the Investor Stock Simulator; it is recommended for anyone under the age of 18 to get their parent's or guardian's permission to use the site's simulator.*

EXERCISE 31

Matching – Match the correct definition with the correct term:

1. Money manager	a. Investments in mutual funds
2. Equity funds	b. Funds made up of bonds
3. Capital gain	c. Group of stocks, bonds, or other securities
4. Money market funds	d. Funds of short-term debt securities
5. Diversification	e. Investment manager for mutual fund
6. Mutual funds	f. Increase in a capital asset
7. Capital	g. Spreading risk among several investments
8. Fixed income funds	h. Funds made up of stocks

LESSON 32 - OTHER INVESTMENTS

There are many other types of investments, including investing in the foreign exchange markets (FOREX), real estate, commodities, art, collectibles, futures, and options (briefly discussed in Lesson 29.) Additionally, there are IRAs and CDs, which we discussed in Lesson 3. Starting a business is also an investment. FOREX, futures, and options are investments that are more complex. It takes an increased knowledge of the securities market to invest in these.

Mailbox money is passive income.

Investing in real estate can be either a passive or a non-passive investment. Let's take a moment to review passive and non-passive income from Lesson 2. When the investment is passive, the investor puts very little or no time into the investment activity. For example, an investor who purchases a commercial or residential property to earn income from leasing the property may use a management company to manage the property. The management company is responsible for negotiating the lease with the tenants, maintaining the property, and collecting rents. Once rent is received, the management company takes their percentage and sends the remainder to the investor. This is referred to as **mailbox money** in the finance industry. Since the investor does not actively participant in the management of the property, this is **passive income**.

On the other hand, some investors are actively involved in the leasing, management, and rent collection activities associated with property ownership. The income earned in this situation is **non-passive income**.

It is important to note investments come with different levels of risk. Some investors are okay with risk, while others are **risk adverse**. A risk adverse investor is one who does not want to lose much or any money in an investment. They prefer to invest in products with a lower return on their investment for the assurance they will not lose any money. Riskier investments tend to have higher returns, but there is a higher probability the investor will lose some of their money. Sometimes, they lose all of their money in a particular investment.

Investors who are risk adverse prefer CDs and money-market savings accounts, while investors with a higher tolerance for investment risk will gravitate toward stocks, collectibles, commodities, FOREX, and timeshares.

The following illustration demonstrates the difference between low and high risk.

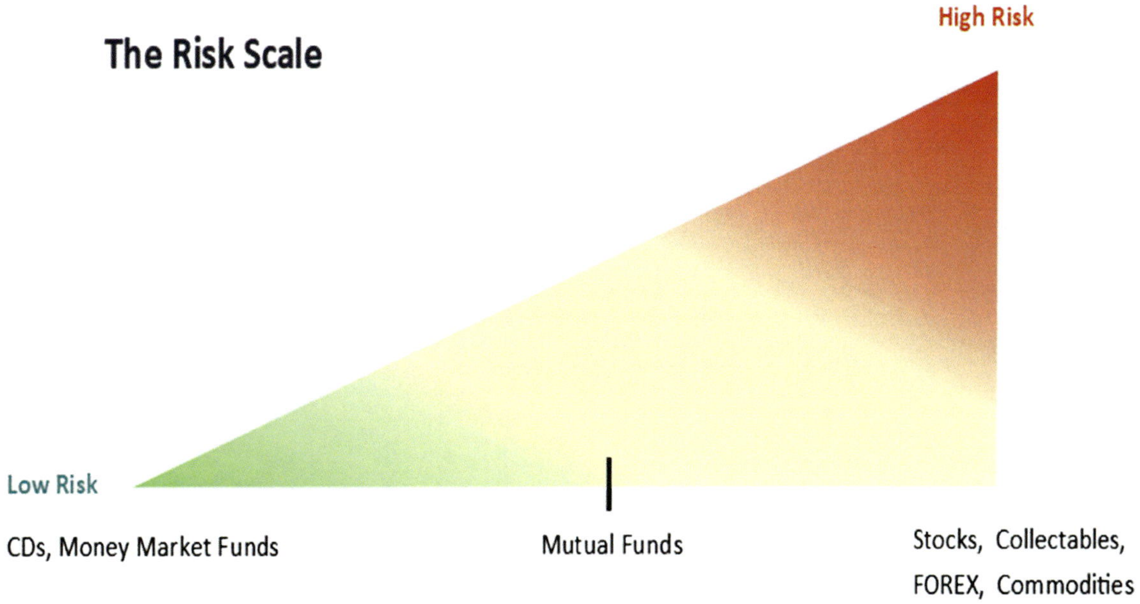

Each investor has to determine their tolerance for investment risk and then chose the investment product that matches. It is recommended that investors have a diverse portfolio that has investments with varying levels of risk.

Make sure to understand the risks associated with each investment!

EXERCISE 32

True or False:

1. True of False. Passive income is earned by actively participating in the investment.

2. True of False. An example of an investment that has increased risk would be stocks.

3. True of False. An investor who is risk adverse is someone who has a low tolerance for losing money on investments.

4. True of False. Mailbox money is a type of non-passive income.

5. True of False. Examples of investments with low to no risk would be IRAs and CDs.

6. True of False. FOREX stands for Foreign Exchange Market.

7. True of False. An investor who manages their real estate investment earns non-passive income.

8. True of False. Investments should not be diversified with high and low risk Investment products.

9. True of False. Each investor has to determine their tolerance for investment risk.

10. True of False. Starting a business not a type of investment.

QUIZ - SECTION 8

Multiple Choice Problems:

1. The acronym for the New York Stock Exchange is:
    a. NYSE
    b. NYSTE
    c. NYMEX
    d. FOREX

2. A type of stock where the shareholder usually does not have the voting rights is:
    a. Common stock
    b. Preferred stock
    c. Mutual stock
    d. Money market stock

3. A type of stock where the shareholder usually does have voting rights:
    a. Mutual stock
    b. Preferred stock
    c. Common stock
    d. Money market stock

4. The money paid from profits to shareholders is called a:
    a. Monthly payment
    b. Dividend
    c. Common stock
    d. Surplus

5. When a company goes out of business and sells all of their assets they have ____________________ their business:
    a. hawked
    b. peddled
    c. sold
    d. liquated

6. A shareholder is a person who:
    a. owes stock in a business.
    b. owes stock to a business.
    c. owns stock in a business.
    d. owns a business.

7. A person who pays for securities in order to get a higher return than what they originally invested is referred to as a(n):
    a. investor
    b. owner
    c. wise person
    d. dedicated

8. Examples of commodities exchanges are the:
    a. New York Mercantile Exchange, Inc., and the New York Stock Exchange.
    b. New York Stock Exchange and the Commodity Exchange, Inc.
    c. New York Mercantile Exchange, Inc., and Chicago Board of Trade (CBOT)
    d. New York Mercantile Exchange, Inc., and the American Stock Exchange.

9. When a person has the right to buy or sell a stock for a set period of time and at a set price they have a (n):
    a. promise
    b. call
    c. put
    d. option

10. When a person has a right to buy a stock they have a:
    a. promise
    b. call option
    c. put option
    d. dividend

11. When a person has a right to sell a stock they have a:
    a. promise
    b. call option
    c. put option
    d. dividend

12. Financial instruments that are sold and purchased by investors in the financial markets are called:
    a. securities
    b. investments
    c. expenses
    d. dividends

13. The three types of bonds are:
    a. corporate, municipal, and governmental.
    b. corporate, state, and governmental.
    c. corporate, municipal, and stock.
    d. corporate, utility, and governmental.

14. The owner of a bond is called a:
    a. bondholder
    b. stockholder
    c. shareholder
    d. debtholder

15. Bonds having a ________________ ________________ to measure a company's ability to pay back their debts:
    a. score system.
    b. rating system.
    c. grade system.
    d. evaluation system.

16. A _______________ _______________ is the difference between how much an investor paid for a bond and how much they made at maturity:
    a. bond margin
    b. bond spread
    c. bond yield
    d. bond range

17. The three most respected bond rating agencies are:
    a. Standard & Poor's, Moody's, and Finch.
    b. Standard Bonds, Moody's, and Fitch.
    c. Standard & Moody's, Poor's, and Fitch.
    d. Standard & Poor's, Moody's, and Fitch.

18. Bonds traded using some other tool than the stock exchanges are called:
    a. over-the-exchange.
    b. over-the-counter.
    c. after-the-exchange.
    d. beyond-the exchange.

19. A ____________________ ____________________ ____________________ changes over the period of a loan:
    a. variable interest rate
    b. fixed interest rate
    c. moveable interest rate
    d. adaptable interest rate

20. A ____________________ ____________________ ____________________ remains the same over the period of a loan:
    a. variable interest rate
    b. fixed interest rate
    c. moveable interest rate
    d. adaptable interest rate

21. A ____________________ ____________________ is comprised of a group of stocks, bonds, and other securities owned by different shareholders:
    a. communal fund
    b. mutual investment
    c. mutual fund
    d. communal investment

22. An increase in a capital asset is called a:
    a. increased income.
    b. increased gain.
    c. increased asset.
    d. capital gain.

23. The money a person or company has invested in order to generate income is called:
    a. wealth.
    b. principal.
    c. capital.
    d. resources.

24. Passive income that an investor receives when they do not participate in an investment is often called:
    a. mailbox money.
    b. easy money.
    c. letterbox money.
    d. mail-drop money.

25. An investor with a low tolerance for losing money in an investment is called:
    a. investment shy.
    b. risk adverse.
    c. risk tolerant.
    d. risk forbearing.

SECTION 9 - LOANS ~ PART I

KEYWORDS

Amortization schedule

Available balance

Borrower

Closed-end loan

Co-borrower

Collateral

Defaults

Guarantors

Lender

Living beyond one's means

Open-end loan

Principal

Revolving loan

Secured loan

Source of cash

Unsecured loans

LEARNING OBJECTIVES FOR SECTION 9

Upon successful completion of Section 9, you will be able to:

- Distinguish between a secured loan from an unsecured loan.
- Calculate a loan payment.

LESSON 33 - SECURED LOANS

When you obtain a **secured loan**, you pledge an asset against the loan. When you borrow money, you are known as the **borrower** and the financial institution or person lending the money is known as the lender. The pledged asset is known as **collateral**. For example, if you purchase a house or car, you pledge the house or car being purchased as collateral for the loan. The most common types of secured loans are home loans, auto loans, recreational vehicle loans, and boat loans.

The purpose of collateral is to lessen the risk to the lender. If you default on your loan, the lender can decrease the money they lose by selling the collateral and paying the monies received against the loan. A borrower **defaults** on a loan when they fall behind on their payments or completely stopped making loan payments.

Less common secured loans occur when a borrower uses cash, CDs, or securities as collateral. With these loans, the collateral pledged for the loan is locked and the borrower cannot access the collateral until the loan is paid and the financial institution releases the collateral.

Sometimes a borrower is required to pledge several pieces of collateral for a loan. This usually occurs when: 1) the borrower does not have any or enough money to put toward the loan as a down payment, 2) the financial institution concludes the borrower is a high risk due to being at their job for a short period of time, 3) the borrower has a lower than desired credit score, or 4) the borrower has late payments on other loans.

Some loans have co-borrowers, also known as obligors. A **co-borrower** is second borrower on a loan and has an equal obligation to pay the loan as does the borrower. Co-borrowers are needed when a borrower does not qualify for the loan on their own.

Co-borrowers are responsible for paying the loan if the borrower defaults!

Other loans have a guarantor, also known as a signatory. **Guarantors** are different than co-borrowers in that the guarantor signs on behalf of the borrower and is not liable for the loan until the borrower defaults. A co-borrower is responsible for repayment of the loan from the start of the loan. Also, the financial institution does not request payment from them unless the borrower defaults on the loan. At the time of the default, the financial institution will either request the guarantor to makes payments or pay the loan in full, whichever is agreed upon at the time of the loan. A difference between co-borrowers and guarantors is that co-borrowers have a right to use and enjoy the goods purchased with the loan and guarantors do not. Additionally, guarantors are common with business loans and not as much with personal loans. Co-borrowers are common on both business and personal loans.

EXERCISE 33

Multiple Choice Problems:

1. When a borrower stops making payments on their loan, they have:
    a. dodged their loan.
    b. defaulted on their loan.
    c. avoided their loan.
    d. sidestepped their loan.

2. A co-borrower:
    a. is not obligated to pay back the loan.
    b. is equally responsible for a loan with the borrower from the start of the loan term.
    c. can choose if they want to pay back the loan or not.
    d. is only partially responsible for paying back the loan.

3. The person who signs on behalf of a borrower and is not obligated on the loan until the borrower defaults is known as a:
    a. backer.
    b. co-borrower.
    c. guarantor.
    d. sponsor.

4. A __________________ __________________ is one that has collateral:
    a. secured loan
    b. unsecured loan
    c. confident loan
    d. None of these

5. An asset that is used to secure a loan is known as:
    a. assurance.
    b. a guarantee.
    c. security.
    d. collateral.

6. A __________________ has full rights to the products purchased:
    a. guarantor
    b. family member
    c. co-borrower
    d. friend

7. The financial institution who is lending money to a borrower is known as the:
    a. lender.
    b. borrower.
    c. co-borrower.
    d. guarantor.

8. A borrower can miss ______________ payments and not be in default:
    a. 1
    b. 0
    c. 2
    d. 3

9. Common secured loans are:
    a. home loans.
    b. auto loans.
    c. boat loans.
    d. All of the above.

10. A loan can have up to ____________________ co-borrowers on a loan:
    a. 1
    b. 4
    c. 6
    d. There is no limit to the number of co-borrowers.

LESSON 34 - UNSECURED LOANS

Unsecured loans are the opposite of secured loans in that these loans do not have any collateral protection. Unsecured loans are considered to be of higher risk to lenders and usually have higher interest rates, higher monthly payments, or both.

Some types of unsecured loans, or debt, are lines of credit, credit cards, payday loans, loans for medical bills, student loans, and signature loans. Government student loans are an anomaly. While these are a type of unsecured loan, many financial institutions view them as a secured loan when running debt ratios because they have a guarantee from the U.S. government.

Credit cards should not be used as a source of cash!

The most difficult type of unsecured debt for a consumer to pay off is credit card debt. Credit cards are an open-end loan from a financial institution. An **open-end loan** is a revolving loan. **Revolving loans** do not have a maturity date and the borrower can continue to borrow on the loan up to the credit limit. The borrower can continue to borrow over and over as the loan is paid down. They do this by using the available balance. The **available balance** is the difference between the credit limit and the outstanding balance. Without a maturity date, a borrower does not know when their open-end loan will be paid off. Another type of open-end loan is a line of credit. **Closed-end loans**, such as house or auto loan, have a maturity date, and the paid down portion of the loan is not available to the borrower.

The credit card payment structure is designed so that the borrower pays a large portion toward interest and a minimal amount toward principal each month. **Principal** is the amount borrowed or owed on a loan. This keeps the principal close to the same amount each month with the borrower not making any real progress toward paying down the principal amount. Why do financial institutions offer these types of loans? First, there is a demand for them by consumers. Second, financial institutions are a business, and like any business, they need to generate revenue. Interest payments on credit cards creates a steady stream of revenue for the credit card issuer. Financial institutions need revenue to continue to operate.

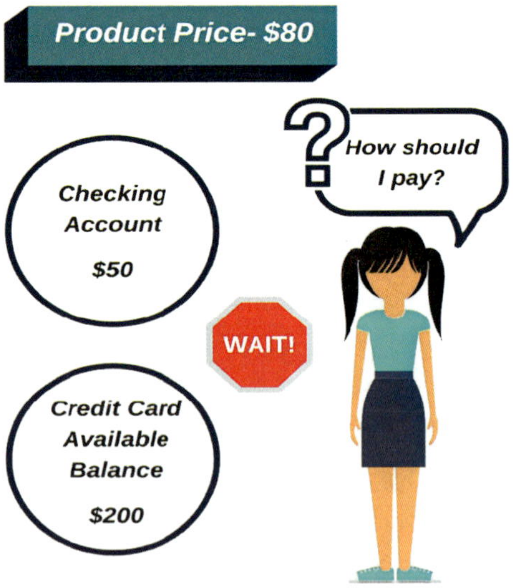

Is there cash available?

Design concept created by Angela K. Love, illustration created by Laura Sullins of Studio Sullins Designs.

An additional struggle with credit cards is that many consumers use them as a source of cash. This happens when a consumer uses their credit cards for purchases when they have no available cash. It is better to wait to purchase products when cash is available than to use credit cards as a **source of cash**. When a borrower does not pay off their credit cards each month, they create a continual cycle of credit card balances remaining the same or increasing each month. Eventually, the monthly payment for a credit card becomes easier to make than the total amount of the expenses being incurred. Once a borrower uses the credit card to its credit limit, they have to decide if they will stop using the credit card or try to get another one. They also have to determine

Try to live within your monthly income.

how to repay the credit card debt they have accumulated. Many consumers, who are now stuck in a credit card spending and debt cycle, get another credit card. This cycle is called **living beyond one's means**.

Overall, credit cards take a long time to pay off if no additional debt is incurred and only the minimum payment is made each month. A hefty amount of interest is paid for the convenience of using a credit card. Credit card issuers make this possible by setting the minimum payment at a low percentage (1 to 3.5%) of the outstanding balance.

The illustration on the right is a sample credit card amortization. An **amortization schedule** is a table that shows how a loan is slowly paid off or how an investment increases in value over time. This is an example of a credit card with a $5,000 outstanding balance, with and interest rate of 14.99%, and a monthly payment requirement of 2% of the outstanding balance. As illustrated, after 120 payments, or 10 years, with no additional debt incurred, there remains an outstanding balance of $2,023.92 with $4,951.32 paid in interest (almost the entire amount of credit charged) and only $2,976.08 paid toward principal. If the same credit card loan maintained a payment of $100 each month, it would take 79 months, or nearly 8 years, to pay off the credit card. The combination of a high-interest rate and adjusting monthly payment results in the credit card debt continuing for years and years.

CREDIT CARD AMORIZATION SCHEDULE EXAMPLE

Payment Number	Payment	Interest	Principal	Balance
				5,000.00
1	100.00	62.46	37.54	4,962.46
2	99.25	61.99	37.26	4,925.20
3	98.50	61.52	36.98	4,888.22
4	97.76	61.06	36.70	4,851.52
5	97.03	60.60	36.43	4,815.09
6	96.30	60.15	36.15	4,778.94
7	95.58	59.70	35.88	4,743.05
8	94.86	59.25	35.61	4,707.44
9	94.15	58.80	35.35	4,672.10
10	93.44	58.36	35.08	4,637.02
11	92.74	57.92	34.82	4,602.20
12	92.04	57.49	34.55	4,567.65
24	84.08	52.52	31.57	4,172.68
36	76.81	47.98	28.84	3,811.86
48	70.17	43.83	26.34	3,482.25
60	64.10	40.04	24.07	3,181.14
72	58.56	36.58	21.98	2,906.06
84	53.50	33.41	20.08	2,654.77
96	48.87	30.52	18.35	2,425.21
108	44.65	27.88	16.76	2,215.50
120	40.78	25.47	15.31	2,023.92
	7,927.39	**4,951.32**	**2,976.08**	

Credit cards are a convenient and useful financial tool IF they are paid off each month. A credit card is a useful tool for traveling. It is not recommended to carry large sums of cash or use debit cards while traveling for security reasons. Stolen cash cannot be replaced, and it is more difficult to replace funds from fraudulent transactions on debit cards than on credit cards. Credit card issuers offer great loyalty programs, and it is tempting to use a credit card for purchases. The loyalty programs are great for those who pay off their outstanding balance each month, but for those who do not, credit card debt can be a tremendous financial burden.

EXERCISE 34

Multiple Choice Problems:

1. A loan that does not have a maturity date and the borrower can keep borrowing up to the credit limit is called a ________________ loan:
    a. closed-end
    b. circular
    c. revolving
    d. rotating

2. Another name for a revolving loan is a:
    a. closed-end loan.
    b. open-end loan.
    c. circular loan.
    d. rotating loan.

3. A loan with a maturity date is a:
    a. closed-end loan.
    b. open-end loan.
    c. revolving loan.
    d. rotating loan.

4. The difference between the credit limit and the outstanding balance is the:
    a. untaken balance.
    b. available balance.
    c. credit balance.
    d. presented balance.

5. Unsecured loans are loans:
    a. that sometimes will have collateral.
    b. that have collateral.
    c. that do not have any collateral.
    d. All of the above.

6. Many borrowers use credit cards as:
    a. a source of cash.
    b. a source of increased wealth.
    c. a way to make more money.
    d. a way to earn more cash.

7. An amortization schedule shows:
    a. the increase of a loan balance or the decrease of an investment balance plus interest accrued over time.
    b. the decrease of a loan balance or the increase of an investment balance plus interest accrued over time.
    c. only the decrease of a loan balance over time.
    d. only the increase of an investment balance over time.

8. When a person is spending more than what they make and has to use credit cards for that purpose, they are:
    a. living within their means.
    b. living beyond their means.
    c. both a and b.
    d. neither a or b.

9. The structure of credit card repayment is inherently set up to:
    a. to pay most of the principal balance each month.
    b. work just like a short-term loan.
    c. take just a few months to pay off.
    d. take many years to pay off.

10. The best use of a credit card is to:
    a. use it for everyday living purchases.
    b. have a large outstanding balance.
    c. pay it off each month.
    d. Any of the answers are good.

LESSON 35 - CALCULATING A LOAN PAYMENT

It is beneficial to know how to calculate a loan payment before seeking a loan. This helps with budgeting and setting financial goals. There are many financial calculators online; however, this lesson will demonstrate how to calculate a fixed interest rate loan payment manually. An illustration of the loan payment formula is below with an explanation of the various components.

$$PMT = \frac{PV\ (r/n)}{[1-(1+r/n)^{-t}]}$$

PMT = Payment

PV = Present Value

r = interest rate

n = number of payments in a year

t = total number of payments

Let's calculate a payment by hand. Here are the loan terms:

A 3-year loan for $5,000 at 3% interest. The loan requires monthly payments.

$$PMT = \frac{5{,}000\ (.03/12)}{1-(1+.03/12)^{-36}}$$

Step 1: Write out the problem using the formula.

$$PMT = \frac{5{,}000\ (.0025)}{1-(1.0025)^{-36}}$$

Step 2: Divide .03 by 12 in the numerator. In the dominator, divide .03 by 12, then add it to 1.

$$PMT = \frac{12.50}{1-(0.9140)}$$

Step 3: Multiply 5,000 by .0025 in the numerator. In the dominator, solve for 1..025 to the negative 36 power. On a scientific calculator, key 1.0025, then xy, then 36, then $\pm$, then hit enter. Do NOT use the minus/substraction sign for the $\pm$, make sure to use the negative key. Round to the nearest ten-thousandth.

$$PMT = \frac{12.50}{0.086}$$

Step 4: Subtract 0.9140 from 1 in the dominator.

Step 5: Divide 0.086 by 12.50

$$PMT = 145.35$$

**When using an online loan payment calculator, the answer may be slightly different due to rounding in step 3.*

Now it's time to practice in Exercise 35.1.

EXERCISE 35

Using a scientific or online loan payment calculator*, determine the loan payment for questions 1 - 5. Each loan has monthly payments. Remember, answers between an online calculator and a scientific calculator may be different up to a few dollars due to rounding.

**www.creditkarma.com/calculators/loan is one of many sites offering a loan payment calculator.*

Answers reflect using the loan payment calculator; however, answers using a scientific calculator are in the solutions manual. Answers between a loan payment calculator and scientific calculator may vary by a few cents to a few dollars.

1. What is the monthly loan payment for a 3-year loan for $4,000 at 3% interest: Choose the closest answer.
    a. $116.32
    b. $135.42
    c. $106.69
    d. $98.75

2. What is the monthly loan payment for a 4-year loan for $9,000 at 4% interest: Choose the closest answer.
    a. $179.47
    b. $228.15
    c. $203.21
    d. $198.76

3. A 5-year loan for $17,000 at 5% interest has a monthly loan payment of: Choose the closest answer.
    a. $365.37
    b. $343.16
    c. $320.81
    d. $299.44

4. A 10-year loan for $60,000 at 7% interest has a monthly loan payment of: Choose the closest answer.
    a. $710.89
    b. $696.65
    c. $676.76
    d. $688.29

5. What is the monthly loan payment for a 15-year loan for $120,000 at 6% interest: Choose the closest answer.
    a. $1,012.63
    b. $999.59
    c. $1,234.01
    d. $1,197.43

QUIZ - SECTION 9

Multiple Choice Problems:

1. A ______________________ isn't liable for a loan until the borrower defaults:
    a. co-borrower
    b. borrower
    c. guarantor
    d. lender

2. A revolving loan is also known as a:
    a. open-end loan.
    b. closed-end loan.
    c. encompassing loan.
    d. maturity loan.

3. Frank got a 3-year auto loan for $6,000 at 3% and has to make monthly payments. His monthly payment will be closest to:
    a. $196.64
    b. $174.49
    c. $165.73
    d. $182.34

4. The primary person(s) who borrow money from a financial institution is referred to as:
    a. co-borrower(s).
    b. borrower(s).
    c. guarantor(s).
    d. lender(s).

5. What type of loan doesn't require collateral?
    a. Mortgage loan
    b. Security loan
    c. Secured loan
    d. Unsecured loan

6. Kim got a 10-year mortgage for $76,000 at 5% and has to make monthly payments. Her monthly payment will be closest to:
    a. $806.10
    b. $856.86
    c. $793.84
    d. $789.91

7. Which of the following is a secured loan:
    a. Mortgage loan
    b. Auto loan
    c. Boat loan
    d. All of the above

8. The difference between the credit limit on a credit card and outstanding balance is the:
    a. amount due.
    b. closed balance.
    c. available balance.
    d. non-available balance.

9. Stuart obtained a 4-year auto loan for $11,000 at 2% and has to make monthly payments. His monthly payment will be closest to:
    a. $257.13
    b. $238.65
    c. $229.01
    d. $223.90

10. When a borrower stops making loan payments, they have _________________ on their loan:
    a. cared
    b. respected
    c. strengthen
    d. defaulted

11. The _________________ amount is the what was borrowed or owed on a loan:
    a. principal
    b. interest
    c. major
    d. None of these

12. Becky obtained a 5-year auto loan for $16,000 at 2.50% and has to make monthly payments. Her monthly payment will be closest to:
    a. $272.50
    b. $301.00
    c. $261.73
    d. $283.96

13. All secured loans require:
    a. one co-borrower.
    b. no collateral.
    c. collateral.
    d. two co-borrowers.

14. When a consumer uses credit cards due to no available cash, they are using credit cards as a:
    a. mandatory option.
    b. source of cash.
    c. Both a and b.
    d. None of the above.

15. Richard obtained a 6-year auto loan for $23,000 at 3.25% and has to make monthly payments. His monthly payment will be closest to:
    a. $291.58
    b. $302.03
    c. $352.03
    d. $333.33

SECTION 10 - LOANS ~ PART II

KEYWORDS

Amount owed
Capacity
Capital
Character
Collateral
Conditions
Credit mix
Credit report
Established credit
Five Cs of Credit
New credit
Payment history
Underwriting

LEARNING OBJECTIVES FOR SECTION 10

Upon successful completion of Section 10, you will be able to:

- Describe a creditor's loan approval process.
- Read and understand a credit report.
- Explain the components of a FICO Score.

LESSON 36 - CREDITORS' LOAN APPROVAL PROCESS

Creditors have a process for determining whether to underwrite a loan for a borrower. **Underwriting** a loan simply means a lender analyzes the strength and weaknesses of a borrower's credit history to determine if they should extend credit and puts their findings in writing. They use the Five C's of Credit as their guide when evaluating the financial condition, credit report, credit score, debts, income, and debt ratios of a borrower.

Five C's of Credit
Character
Capital
Capacity
Conditions
Collateral

The **Five C's of Credit** are character, capital, capacity, conditions, and collateral. **Character** is the borrower's willingness to repay their debts. A credit report shows how willing a borrower has been in the past to pay their debts on time.

Capital is how much a borrower is putting down as a deposit toward a loan. The lender wants to know if the borrower is risking any money of their own for the loan they are requesting. Also, capital shows the remaining resources a borrower has after they make the down payment. Those with significant cash in savings or investments are less risky.

Capacity tells the lender if the borrower has enough income to pay the requested debt on time and continuously until the debt has been retired.

Conditions apply to the current economy in the market where the borrower resides. The lender wants to make sure the market is stable for the product being purchased. For example, if a borrower is considering the purchase of a house, the lender wants to be fairly confident the housing market will be stable during the duration of the loan.

Collateral is the capital asset(s) that offer protection for the lender in case the borrower defaults on the loan.

Each financial institution runs a variety of ratios. The most common ratio used for personal loans such as mortgages, auto loans, and credit cards is the debt-to-income (DTI) ratio. The DTI calculates the total recurring debt payments each month divided by total gross monthly income, and it looks like this:

$$\text{DTI} = \frac{\textbf{Total of all Monthly Recurring Debt Payments}}{\textbf{Total Monthly Gross Income}}$$

For example, if the loan is for a car, the lender takes the new potential payment and all other recurring debt payments for each month and adds them together. They would not include payments that will no longer exist within the next one to three months or are not recurring. Then, they divide that number by the borrower's total monthly gross income. The maximum DTI threshold to qualify for a loan is set by each financial institution.

EXAMPLE 36-1

Suppose: Hanna wants to get an auto loan. The lender is calculating Hanna's DTI. Her new auto loan payment would be $250.00, and she has monthly mortgage and student loan payments of $450.00 and $125.00, respectively. Her monthly gross income is $3,000. What is her DTI? Do you think a lender would approve the her loan request?

Answer: Hanna's DTI is 27.50%. Total monthly debt payment of $825 (250 + 450 + 125) / $3,000. Generally, a DTI less than 36% is preferable to lenders. Additionally, a DTI of 28% or less for a mortgage is preferred. Therefore, a total DTI of 27.50% would be acceptable to a lender and Hanna would be approved for the auto loan assuming no other issues are present with her loan application.

Creditors look at all of the information as a whole to determine if a person qualifies for a loan. Forsome loans, such as a mortgage loan, the lender will request a verification of employment and salary to verify the borrower's income. This can sometimes be done by presenting paystubs, but the lender may request a verification of employment from the employer. Each financial institution has different requirements.

In order to obtain a loan at a credit union, the borrower must be a member of the credit union as required by the NCUA regulatory guidelines. Banks typically do not require borrowers to have accounts at their institutions.

EXERCISE 36

Multiple Choice Problems:

1. Which of the following Five C's of Credit shows a borrower's willingness and ability to repay a loan:
    a. Character
    b. Capital
    c. Collateral
    d. Capacity

2. Which of the following describes when a borrower puts down a deposit for a loan:
    a. Collateral
    b. Capacity
    c. Capital
    d. Conditions

3. When a lender evaluates the economy and current market conditions, they are looking at:
    a. Character
    b. Conditions
    c. Collateral
    d. Capacity

4. The lender requires ____________________ to protect them in case a borrower defaults on a loan:
    a. Capital
    b. Capacity
    c. Character
    d. Collateral

5. Which of the following is a borrower's ability to repay their debts:
    a. Collateral
    b. Character
    c. Capacity
    d. Conditions

6. Sarah has $1,400 in total monthly recurring debt and $4,600 in total monthly gross income. What is her DTI:
    a. 33.08%
    b. 29.46%
    c. 30.44%
    d. 328.57%

7. Bambi has $1,000 in total monthly recurring debt, $200 in non-recurring debt, and $3,300 in total monthly gross income. What is her DTI:
    a. 36.36%
    b. 30.30%
    c. 330%
    d. 275%

8. Chuck has the following monthly debt payments: $300 for rent, $75 for a student loan, one final payment of $500, and will have a new loan payment of $375. His monthly gross income is $2,400. What is his DTI:
    a. 31.25%
    b. 52.08%
    c. 320%
    d. 312.50%

9. Greg has the following monthly debt payments: $450 for mortgage, $82 for a credit card, one final payment of $250, and will have a new loan payment of $300. His monthly gross income is $1,400. What is his DTI:
    a. 129.39%
    b. 168.27%
    c. 77.29%
    d. 59.43%

10. Kate has the following monthly debt payments: $500 for rent, $125 for a credit card, and she will have a new loan payment of $175. Her monthly gross income is $1,629. What is her DTI:
    a. 49.11%
    b. 260.64%
    c. 38.37%
    d. 203.63%

LESSON 37 - CREDIT REPORT

A **credit report** is a report listing details of an individual's credit history. It shows their history of loans, history of payments, judgments, liens, and any bankruptcies. It also shows their current and former addresses. Additionally, it lists the date and financial institution of any credit reports that have been requested in the past 45 days. When a lender sees a list of financial institutions that have requested a credit report for a borrower within a short period of time, they usually suspect the borrower has been turned down for the requested loan by other institutions.

Lenders will discuss the credit report with the borrower but will not give a copy of the credit report to the borrower. This is usually because the financial institution pays a fee for each credit report they request; therefore, they own the credit report. If the borrower thinks there is an error on their credit report, the lender is not able to make any changes or dispute the error.

Consumers who think there are any discrepancies on their credit report should write the reporting agency and dispute any information they think is in error. Borrowers who are denied credit will be mailed an opportunity to request their credit report. According to the Fair Credit Reporting Act (FCRA), each credit bureau is required to provide every consumer, 18 years and older, a free copy of their report once a year upon request. This report must be requested as the credit bureaus do not send reports to consumers automatically. Each credit reporting agency (credit bureaus) offers a free copy as does Credit Karma (creditkarma.com) and AnnualCreditReport.com. The websites for the three main credit bureaus are experian.com for Experian, transunion.com for Transunion, and equifax.com for Equifax. If a website requests a form of payment, the consumer should request their credit report from a different site.

A credit report is a record of a person's financial history.

The three most popular credit bureaus (listed in no particular order) for personal credit reports are Experian, Equifax, and TransUnion. Each reporting agency has a different format for their credit reports; however, they report most of the same information, and all three agencies report a FICO score. (FICO scores will be discussed in Lesson 38.) When married couples apply for a loan together, financial institutions will request a combined credit report.

When lenders review a credit report, they are assessing a person's character. They try to answer the following questions:

- Has the borrower shown a willingness and ability to pay back their debts on time?
- Does the borrower have any loan defaults?
- How many times has the borrower applied for credit in the past 45 days?
- Does the borrower have a significant amount of debt compared to their income?

Creditors use credit reports to verify the current address and credit history of a borrower. When a borrower applies for a loan, they are required to list their debts. This list of debts should match the credit report. Private loans, such as from family members, will not show up on a credit report; however, these loans should still be disclosed to the lender. Below is an illustration of a credit report.

Credit reports can be quite intimating when viewed for the first time. It is important to look at the report section by section and read it thoroughly. If something does not make sense or appears to be in error, contact the credit bureau that created the report using their contact information on the report or their website.

————————————Logo or Header Information for Credit Bureau / Report Number————————————

Name **Social Security Number (SSN)** **Date of Birth**

Current Address **Phone Number**

Former Address

Current Employer & Address

Special messages or negative items are listed here such as ID Alert, Fraud Alert, SSN Problems, Bankruptcies, Liens, Garnishments, Court Orders, collections, etc. Any type of credit/financial issues are typically listed here. Any disputes or statements made by the consumer are listed with the issue in question.

The FICO score is usually listed here.

List of loans are listed next.
Each loan will have the following information:
Loan Holder Name (e.g. Discover, Chase, Financial Institution) **Account/Credit Card Number**
Address
Phone Number
Status: Comments made by the loan holder.

Date Opened: ***01/2015***	**Type of account (revolving or installment)** ***e.g. revolving or installment***	**Credit Limit or Original Amount of the Loan:** ***Dollar amount for the loan or credit card***
Reported Since: ***03/2015***	**Terms:** ***36 months or revolving***	**High Balance:** ***Loan starting balance or highest credit card balance***
Date of Status: ***03/2015***	**Monthly Payment:** ***$200***	**Recent Balance:** ***Most recent balance of the loan***
Last Reported: ***03/2015***	**Recent Payment:** ***Dollar amount of most recent payment.***	

List of credit report requests, listing name of the creditor and the date the request was made.
Any creditor that has requested a credit report in the past 45 days is listed here. This shows a creditor if a consumer is shopping a loan and can be a red flag for possible rapid increase of new loan debt.

Some credit bureau reports list the consumer current and former address, SSN, date of birth, and employment information here instead of at the beginning of the report.

Any formal statements submitted to the credit bureau, such as disputing a collection or explaining the circumstances of late payments, by the consumer regarding their credit report are listed here.

EXERCISE 37

Fill in the Blanks:

1. A ______________________ ______________________ lists the credit history of an individual.

2. The three most popular credit bureaus are ______________________, ______________________, and ______________________.

3. Lenders use credit reports to check the ______________________ of a borrower.

4. If a borrower is ______________________ a loan, they will receive a letter in the mail from the credit bureaus.

5. Lenders ______________________ ______________________ give a borrower a copy of their credit report.

6. Every person who is 18 years old or older can receive a ______________________ copy of their credit report ______________________ a year.

7. If a person thinks there is a ______________________ on their credit report, they can ______________________ it by writing the credit bureaus.

8. Each agency gives a ______________________ score on each credit report.

9. Credit reports list the history of requested credit reports for the past ______________________ days.

10. Lenders compare the list of debts on a credit report to the ______________________ given by the borrower.

LESSON 38 - FICO SCORE

FICO scores are used by creditors to evaluate a borrower's credit history and to determine if they will extend credit to a particular borrower. FICO Scores are based on five components on a 100% scale:

- 35% is based on payment history
- 30% is based on the amount owed
- 15% is based on the length of the credit history
- 10% is based on new credit obtained, and
- 10% has to do with credit mix.

Each financial institution uses a rating system to extend credit. Many financial institutions use a risk-based rating scale for personal loans, which means they extend credit based on a borrower's FICO score and determine the interest rate based on which risk category a borrower's FICO score falls into. The rating categories are "A," "B," "C," "D," "E," and "R." An "R" rating means the borrower needs to restore or rebuild their credit before obtaining any sort of credit.

RISK BASED RATING SCALE EXAMPLE FOR 36 MONTH AUTO LOAN USING FICO SCORE TO DETERMINE BORROWER'S INTEREST RATE

RATING	FICO SCORE	Interest Rate*
"A" Rating	725 - HIGHER	2.45%
"B" Rating	685-724	2.70%
"C" Rating	640-684	4.35%
"D" Rating	600-639	8.90%
"E" Rating	550-599	13.50%
"RESTORE" Rating	549 - BELOW	18.00%

**This is only an example. Interest rates vary by term, type of loan, and institution.*

The illustration to the left shows an example of a financial institution's rating system based on a borrower's FICO score. Each institution using a risk-based rating scale determines the ranges for each of their ratings. Additionally, some institutions use words like "premier" or "premium" instead of "A Rate" or "B Rate" to define their ranges.

The **amount owed** applies not only to the total amount owed, but to a ratio of how much credit is available to the borrower to how much is currently borrowed. For example, Mazie may have $2,000 in available credit, but only have $500 in outstanding balances. Many people think that paying off their credit card each month will improve their FICO score, but it usually does not. Here's why. Each month, creditors report information about their loans with each borrower to one, two, or all three of the credit bureaus. They report the outstanding balance, but the borrower may pay their balance to zero after the financial institution sends their reports to the credit bureaus. Thus, it could appear that a borrower has high balances or have maxed out their credit cards. To keep this situation from negatively affecting a person's FICO score, the borrower needs to keep their total amount of outstanding loan balances at 30% or lower of the total available money to them. For example, if you have a credit card with a $1,000 credit limit, you should not have a balance of more than $300 on the card.

The **new credit** component of the FICO score rates how much new credit a person has recently received. If a person applying for an auto loan has two recently opened credit cards, the financial institution may consider them a high credit risk.

The FICO score includes how long an individual has had **established credit**. If you are new to getting loans, this is reflected in your score. The longer you have credit and pay on time, the higher your score will be.

Payment history is very important. While cell phone, utility, and medical bills do not show up on credit reports if they are paid on time, they will show up on a credit report if a person becomes delinquent and the bill is sent to a collection agency. Delinquent payments that show up on a credit report have the largest impact (35%) on a FICO score.

The final component of the FICO score is the credit mix. The **credit mix** is the combination of loans a person has, which is the mix of secured and unsecured debt. In order to approve a house loan, many financial institutions require borrowers to have a history of different types of credit in which they have made timely payments. Also, lenders look for a certain number of both secured and unsecured loans. Each financial institution has a different set of criteria but the criteria are quite similar.

A good FICO score takes a lot of hard work to earn!

EXERCISE 38

Multiple Choice Problems:

1. A person's outstanding credit to available credit should be kept at:
    a. 30% or less.
    b. 40% or less.
    c. 50% or less.
    d. It doesn't matter.

2. A FICO score is on based on ________________ components:
    a. 2
    b. 6
    c. 5
    d. 1

3. Payment history represents ____________________% of a person's FICO score:
    a. 20
    b. 25
    c. 10
    d. 35

4. Credit mix is the:
    a. combination of multiple payments.
    b. combination of the secured and unsecured debt on a person's credit report.
    c. how much credit a person has over time.
    d. None of these.

5. _________________ ________________ rates how much new credit a person has recently received:
    a. Old credit
    b. New credit
    c. Payment history
    d. Credit mix

6. The component of the FICO score are:
    a. amount owed, new credit, length of credit history, and payment history.
    b. amount owed, new credit, payment history, and credit mix.
    c. amount owed, new credit, length of credit history, payment history, and credit mix.
    d. amount owned, old credit, length of credit history, payment history, and credit mix.

7. Risk based lending:
    a. is when a lender extends a loan to borrower without a FICO score.
    b. is when a lender based the interest rate for a loan on the borrower's FICO score.
    c. is when a lender decides to give the same interest rate for a loan to everyone.
    d. None of these.

8. Financial institutions who use risk based lending typically use:
    a. A, B, C, D, E, and R rates.
    b. A, B, C, D, E, and F rates.
    c. A, B, C, D, F, and R rates.
    d. A, B, D, E, F, and R rates.

9. Established credit defines:
    a. how many mortgages are on a borrower's credit report.
    b. the type of different credit for a borrower.
    c. the credit history of a borrower.
    d. All of the above.

10. Every lending institution:
    a. never changes their interest rates.
    b. uses government designated interest rates.
    c. has the exact same interest rates.
    d. decides their interest rates.

QUIZ - SECTION 10

Multiple Choice Problems:

1. Charlie has the following monthly debt payments: $500 for rent, $135 for a student loan, one final payment of $700, and will have a new loan payment of $475. His monthly gross income is $2,900. What is his DTI:
    a. 160.22%
    b. 38.28%
    c. 62.41%
    d. 57.76%

2. The Five C's of Credit are:
    a. Character, capital, capacity, conditions, and collateral.
    b. Capital, capacity, conditions, collateral, and charm.
    c. Character, capability, capital, conditions, and collateral.
    d. Character, capital, capacity, circumstances, and collateral.

3. A credit report:
    a. is a report listing credit possibilities for a borrower.
    b. is a report listing the details of a person's credit history.
    c. is a report listing a person's work experience.
    d. None of the above.

4. Bill has the following monthly debt payments: $1,200 for rent, $298 for a credit card, one final payment of $600, and will have a new loan payment of $375. His monthly gross income is $4,600. What is his DTI:
    a. 186.00%
    b. 245.60%
    c. 40.72%
    d. 53.76%

5. The five categories of a FICO score are:
    a. amount owned, new credit, length of credit history, payment history, and credit mix.
    b. amount owed, old credit, length of credit history, payment history, and credit mix.
    c. amount owed, new credit, length of credit history, payment history, and credit variations.
    d. amount owed, new credit, length of credit history, payment history, and credit mix.

6. The three most popular credit bureaus are:
    a. Experian, Equifax, and SubUnion.
    b. Experian, EquiNow, and TransUnion.
    c. Equifax, Experian, and TransUnion.
    d. Equifax, ExperFICO, and TransUnion.

7. Sally has the following monthly debt payments: $750 for mortgage, $94 for a credit card, one final payment of $225, and will have a new loan payment of $333. Her monthly gross income is $2,345. What is her DTI:
    a. 50.19%
    b. 59.79%
    c. 45.59%
    d. 55.78%

8. The payment history on a FICO score rates:
    a. how many payments a borrower made in the last year.
    b. how well a borrower has made payments in the past.
    c. how well a borrower will make payments in the future.
    d. All of the above.

9. The DTI ratio is calculated by:
    a. multiplying total of all monthly recurring debt payments by total monthly gross income.
    b. dividing total of all monthly recurring debt payments by total monthly gross income.
    c. dividing total monthly gross income by total of all monthly recurring debt payments.
    d. subtracting total monthly gross income from total of all monthly recurring debt payments.

10. Kari has the following monthly debt payments: $525 for mortgage, $125 for a two-year personal loan, one final payment of $235, and will have a new loan payment of $200. Her monthly gross income is $2,756. What is her DTI:
    a. 32.11%
    b. 20.32%
    c. 34.83%
    d. 30.84%

11. A borrower's list of debts on a loan application should:
    a. match the list of debts on their credit report.
    b. also list everyday expenses such as groceries.
    c. only list their rent or mortgage payment.
    d. None of the above.

12. Each financial institution:
    a. uses the government standard interest rates for auto loans.
    b. copies their competitor's rates.
    c. has their own set of interest rates.
    d. uses the state interest rates published each morning.

13. Tom has the following monthly debt payments: $684 for mortgage, $135 for a student loan, $125 for a credit card, and will have a new loan payment of $196. His monthly gross income is $3,679. What is his DTI:
    a. 30.99%
    b. 27.59%
    c. 27.32%
    d. 23.92%

14. Underwriting a loan means:
    a. a lender analyzes the strength and weaknesses of a lender's credit history to determine if they should extend credit and puts their findings in writing
    b. a lender analyzes the accomplishments of a borrower's credit history to determine if they should extend credit and puts their findings in writing
    c. a lender analyzes the strength and weaknesses of a borrower's work history to determine if they should extend credit and puts their findings in writing
    d. a lender analyzes the strength and weaknesses of a borrower's credit history to determine if they should extend credit and puts their findings in writing.

15. FICO scores in risk based lending institutions determines:
    a. which payment a borrower will make on their loan.
    b. which interest rate a borrower qualifies.
    c. how many co-borrowers there should be on a loan.
    d. All of the above.

UNIT II TEST

Multiple Choice Problems:

1. Not-for-profit organizations earn profits:
    a. for their owners/members.
    b. and invest them back into their organizations to meet their goals.
    c. for consumers.
    d. to pay huge salaries to CEO.

2. ATM cards can be used:
    a. at ATM machines and to make purchases.
    b. only to make purchases.
    c. only at ATM machines to deposit and withdraw money.
    d. only inside a financial institution.

3. Savings and checking accounts are usually insured:
    a. up to $250,000 for each depositor either by the FDIC for credit unions or by the NCUA for banks.
    b. up to $250,000 for each depositor either by the FDIC for banks or by the NCUA for credit unions.
    c. up to $150,000 for each account either by the FDIC for credit unions or by the NCUA for banks.
    d. up to $150,000 for each depositor either by the FDIC for credit unions or by the NCUA for banks.

4. In a check register, WD stands for:
    a. withholding deposit.
    b. withdrawal.
    c. wait deposit.
    d. None of these.

5. Shareholders:
    a. can only purchase common stocks.
    b. do not purchase or sell stocks.
    c. are investors who used to hold shares in a company, but sold them.
    d. are investor who hold shares, or ownership, of a company with stocks that they purchase.

6. The owner of a bond is a:
    a. debtholder.
    b. bondholder.
    c. bondsperson.
    d. bond debtor.

7. Fixed-income funds:
    a. invest in both U.S. and global stocks.
    b. are typically comprised of short-term debt securities.
    c. are made up of corporate, municipal, and federal bonds.
    d. are only made up of treasury bills.

8. FOREX stands for:
   a. future exchange markets.
   b. foundational markets.
   c. foreign exchange markets.
   d. None of these.

9. All secured loans have:
   a. high monthly payments.
   b. collateral.
   c. low monthly payments.
   d. short loan terms.

10. Revolving loans:
   a. variable maturity dates.
   b. fixed maturity dates.
   c. have a 24-month maturity date.
   d. do not have a maturity date.

11. What is the monthly loan payment for a 7-year loan for $46,000 at 6% interest: Choose the closest answer.
   a. $671.99
   b. $699.99
   c. $703.76
   d. $653.64

12. The character of a borrower measures:
   a. how much they are willing to put down as a deposit for a loan.
   b. their willingness to pay their debts.
   c. the value of a borrower's capital asset.
   d. All of these.

13. Financial institutions run a credit report:
   a. only if a borrower doesn't have a co-borrower.
   b. rarely.
   c. almost any time a person wants to borrow money.
   d. every other time a person borrows money.

14. FICO scores:
   a. are used by consumers to calculate their monthly loan payments.
   b. are used by creditors to determine a borrower's monthly loan payment.
   c. are used by consumers to measure the interest rates of financial institutions.
   d. are used by creditors to evaluate a borrower's credit history.

15. "Field of membership":
   a. applies to credit unions and not banks.
   b. applies to banks and not credit unions.
   c. applies to both credit unions and banks.
   d. applies to neither banks nor credit unions.

16. A check for $156.94 would be written as which of the following on a check:
    a. One-hundred, fifty six, and 94 cents -------------------------------------
    b. One hundred, fifty-six and ninety-four/100 ----------------------------
    c. One hundred, fifty-six and 94/100 ---------------------------------------
    d. One hundred and fifty-six dollars and 94/100 ------------------------

17. What is the federal limit of withdrawals that can be made from a savings account each month:
    a. 3
    b. 10
    c. 4
    d. 6

18. Checking and savings accounts should be reconciled:
    a. once a quarter.
    b. once a month.
    c. once a year.
    d. once a week.

19. When a company goes out of business and sells all of its assets, it has:
    a. liquidated.
    b. closed its doors.
    c. settled its accounts.
    d. discharged its assets.

20. An opportunity cost:
    a. is money that is available today.
    b. is that which is lost when one opportunity is chosen over an alternative one.
    c. both a and b are correct.
    d. None of the above.

21. Bond:
    a. had a rating system in the past, but do not any longer.
    b. have never had a rating system.
    c. have a rating system.
    d. None of the above.

22. Mutual funds:
    a. are comprised of stocks owned by only one shareholder.
    b. are comprised only of bonds owned by different shareholders.
    c. are comprised only of a variety of stocks owned by different shareholders.
    d. are comprised of a group of stocks, bonds, and other securities owned by different shareholders.

23. When an investor is sensitive about losing money from investments, they are:
    a. risk savvy.
    b. risk adverse.
    c. risk hostile.
    d. risk shrewd.

24. When a borrower stops making payments on a loan, they have:
    a. a good reason most of the time.
    b. defaulted on their loan.
    c. had increased interest rates making payments impossible.
    d. improved their payment history.

25. Guarantors are:
    a. not liable for a loan until the borrower defaults on the loan.
    b. liable for a loan throughout the entire loan.
    c. not liable for a loan even if the borrower defaults on the loan.
    d. liable for a loan half through the term of the loan.

26. The time value of money states that:
    a. money available tomorrow has more value than the same amount of money today.
    b. money available today that has equal value to the same amount of money in the future.
    c. money available today has less value than the same amount of money in the future.
    d. money available today has more value than the same amount of money in the future.

27. What is the monthly loan payment for a 3-year loan for $6,200 at 4% interest; Choose the closest answer.
    a. $200.09
    b. $192.48
    c. $183.05
    d. $174.91

28. Mitch has the following monthly debt payments: $550 for rent, $68 for a credit card, $160 for student loans, and will have a new loan payment of $175. His monthly gross income is $1,543. What is his DTI:
    a. 26.12%
    b. 51.39%
    c. 57.36%
    d. 61.76%
29. The list of debts a borrower puts down on a loan application should match:
    a. a best guess by the borrower.
    b. their credit report.
    c. decided by the lender.
    d. None of the above.

30. If a borrower thinks their credit report has a discrepancy, they:
    a. tell the lender and have them fix it.
    b. ignore it.
    c. write the credit bureau and dispute the discrepancy.
    d. don't worry about it, because it will eventually disappear.

31. Which of the following is considered cash:
    a. equity in a house.
    b. ownership of a boat.
    c. marketable securities.
    d. money borrowed with a loan to buy a car.

32. A FICO that puts a borrower in the "R" rating category needs to:
    a. work on restoring or rebuilding their credit history.
    b. not worry about a low credit score.
    c. have the lender give them a higher FICO score.
    d. be proud of a high FICO score.

33. Incurring debt:
    a. increases a person's wealth.
    b. does not increase a person's wealth.
    c. always opens up opportunities.
    d. should be done whenever possible.

34. The future value of investing $7,000 at 5% for 10 years, would be closet to:
    a. $11,333.90
    b. $11,873.03
    c. $11,529.07
    d. $11,643.39

35. When a person uses a credit card for everyday expenses because they don't have any cash, they are using the credit card:
    a. until the make more money.
    b. only once.
    c. for necessary reasons.
    d. as a source of cash.

UNIT 3
BEHAVIORAL FINANCE

Learning Objectives

Upon successful completion of this unit, you will be able to do the following:

- Identify financial pitfalls.
- Create a budget.
- Manage a budget.

SECTION 11 - FINANCIAL PITFALLS

KEYWORDS

Need

Want

LEARNING OBJECTIVES FOR SECTION 11

Upon successful completion of Section 11, you will be able to:

- Identify financial pitfalls.
- Characterize healthy financial habits.

LESSON 39 - TREATING "WANTS" LIKE "NEEDS"

One of the most difficult aspects of creating and following a budget is determining which purchases are truly needs and which are only wants. Wanting something can feel much like needing it. Treating a "want" like a "need" can lead to the financial pitfall of increasing debt.

Do not confuse 'wants' with 'needs'.

A **need** is something a person must have to live such as food, water, clothing, shelter, and human interaction. A **want** is a desire for something that is not needed. Sometimes these needs become confused with wants. For example, people need clothing; however, most people do not need expensive brand-named clothing. The same is true for food, water, and shelter. Buying groceries and cooking instead of eating out and drinking tap water (filtered if necessary) instead of buying bottled water saves a lot of money. Buying or renting a home based on one's budget rather than following a desire for status also goes a long way toward avoiding financial pitfalls.

To separate needs from wants, a person should make a list of everything they think they will spend money on in a given month, including what is already being spent. Then the list of those items should be divided into needs (what a person must have) and wants (what can be let go of or purchased in the future). Below is an illustration of a list of monthly purchases (left column). The list of purchases is divided into needs (middle column), wants (right column), and ideas of how to curb costs.

LIST OF MONTHLY PURCHASES	NEEDS	WANTS
• Eating out with friends	• Food - eating with friends can be done through entertaining at home.	• Eating out with friends
• Groceries	• Clothing/shoes—the biggest savings are gained when buying off season (e.g. buying winter clothes in February and summer clothes in August).	• Expensive clothing and shoes
• Clothing	• Personal Care	• Accessories
• Shoes	• Gasoline	• Movies—many movie theaters have deals during certain times or days.
• Accessories & Personal Care	• Auto maintenance—oil changes and repairs	• Video games, magazines, books—look for used games or limit number of purchases to a certain number per year.
• Movies	• Auto insurance	• Music—many radio stations offer free streaming.
• Video games	• Entertainment—it's a given people are going to spend time do fun things. Limit events, combine activities, and find inexpensive alternatives.	• Electronics—sometimes certain electronics are needed. Shop deals.
• Music	• Some furniture, such as a bed is needed. Limit purchases.	• Décor for car & bedroom—look for deals, limit purchases, save money for car maintenance.
• Gasoline		• Entertainment—Limit money spent.
• Electronics & Gadgets		• Furniture—Look for deals.
• Magazines & Books		
• Décor for car & bedroom		
• Auto insurance		
• Entertainment		
• Furniture		

"Take care of what you have until you know where your betters are coming from." ~ Agnes Newman

As can be seen, many purchases can be changed to accommodate needs and wants. Most people want to spend time having fun with friends and family. Choosing to buy and prepare food for friends and family in one's home combines a need and a want while lowering costs.

EXERCISE 39

The exercise for this lesson will be to create a list of your current monthly purchases and projected monthly purchases expected in the future in the left column. Then, separate those purchases according to needs and wants in the respective columns.

LIST OF CURRENT AND FUTURE MONTHLY PURCHASES	NEEDS	WANTS
______________	______________	______________
______________	______________	______________
______________	______________	______________
______________	______________	______________
______________	______________	______________
______________	______________	______________
______________	______________	______________
______________	______________	______________
______________	______________	______________
______________	______________	______________
______________	______________	______________
______________	______________	______________
______________	______________	______________
______________	______________	______________
______________	______________	______________
______________	______________	______________
______________	______________	______________
______________	______________	______________
______________	______________	______________

Which purchases were you able to combined to lessen costs? ______________________________

____

____

____

____

LESSON 40 - TAKING ON TOO MUCH DEBT

In this fast paced, technology driven society, it can seem impossible to avoid debt. There are so many attractive things pulling at people's time and financial resources. Before the advent of credit cards and the substantial increase in loan products, many people saved their money to buy toys, go out to eat, go to the movies, buy nice clothes, and more. Since money was not readily available in the form of debt, people went without or were very creative with how they spent their time.

It is easier than ever to take on too much debt. Many financial institutions have increased their ratios, allowing borrowers to have higher debt percentages. Giving into debt means potentially giving up future opportunities. Certain types of debt make sense, for example a home mortgage. If you are paying rent but can get a mortgage for the same monthly payment and can afford house maintenance, then a mortgage is a way to build equity. However, many take on a mortgage payment that is too high even though it fits within the financial institution's ratios.

Living frugally in order to decrease or keep from taking on too much debt should be a first priority. Once you are caught up in a cycle of too much debt, it may seem impossible to get off the wheel of debt. It is possible, though! It takes determination, planning, budgeting, and following the plan and budget. It means saying "no" to wants and figuring out a way to curb spending on needs.

High school students do not have debt and can start off with good financial habits. The following illustration identifies some good financial habits to implement as one starts their financial path:

Do not use credit cards! They are not a source of cash!	Always put a percentage of each paycheck into savings!	Make adjustments to a budget that is not working!	Learn to say ***no*** to wants ... plan for them instead!
Do not borrow to the maximum limit available!	Remember! Debt does not increase wealth!	Live within the parameters of your paycheck!	Be a continual learner of finance!
Do not let mistakes cause discouragement! Keep going!	Create a budget and follow it!	Plan for FUN!	Always have a healthy cushion between income and expenses!

There are many other healthy financial habits, but these are a good place to start!

EXERCISE 40.1

Study the list of healthy financial habits, then write each one here. Refer back to the list if necessary.

1. ______________________________
2. ______________________________
3. ______________________________
4. ______________________________
5. ______________________________
6. ______________________________
7. ______________________________
8. ______________________________
9. ______________________________
10. ______________________________

EXERCISE 40.2

What other healthy financial habits could be added to the list?

____

____

____

____

____

____

____

____

____

LESSON 41 - ATTITUDES TOWARD MONEY

There are many different attitudes toward money. Many books discuss behavioral finance for investors. Behavioral attitudes of investors are discussed with such terms as attitudes of entitlement, free-spirited, problem solver, organized, and unpredictable to list a few.

Those with an entitlement attitude are like lions. Lions spend 16 to 20 hours of their day sleeping; therefore, they have learned how to work smarter, not harder. Even though they may work smarter and not harder, they expect to have whatever they want. Lions dominate and rule their kingdom. This is great for the lion, but not so much for a person. Those with a lion type personality expect everything to be easy and that they will be successful regardless of planning, effort, experience, or education. A person with this attitude has to work on controlling spending, creating and following a budget, and saying no to wants. Working smarter and not harder really occurs when the person creates and follows a budget, controls spending, and acquires the discipline to save for surprise expenses. When debt begins to pile up due to overspending, lion types will have to work harder to pay off the debt and build up savings.

People with free-spirited attitudes toward money are like monkeys. Monkeys are mischievous, show-offs, fun, fun-loving, friendly, and social animals. They would rather play than work. They hang out together in groups. People who have a monkey-like personality love to be the life of the party. They do not value money except as a means to have fun. They are not planners and are not organized. Creating a budget is the last thing they are interested in doing. Those with a free-spirited, monkey type attitude toward money need to work toward disciplining themselves to manage their money. Creating and following a budget will go against who they are as a person, but it is necessary. This personality type should make sure to budget for fun!

Discover your attitude toward money. Work to improve your weaknesses and keep your strengths strong.

Those with problem solver attitudes are like eagles. Eagles are fearless, resolute, problem solvers who love to take on challenges. Like monkeys, they love to put on a show as they soar through the sky. They understand the dangers to their families and work to avoid those dangers by building their nests high up in trees or cliffs close to water. They plan their nest location and have a routine for building their nests, mating, and raising their eaglets. Those who are like eagles value security and understand the risks before them. Eagle types like routine and like to plan, although they will veer off the plan if necessary to obtain a goal. Routine in a budget is good, but it can also be a problem. One must be willing to change what is not working in their budget, but they should never veer off using a budget. Sticking to a budget and following through will bring success in the long-run.

Those with organizer attitudes towards money are like beavers. Beavers are organized, clever, creative, predictable, and disciplined animals. They love to organize their surroundings. They are creative in building their homes. They are also resilient! If their home is destroyed, they build a new one. They never seem to stop working, but they do have fun. They work hard so they can enjoy life and be secure. Beaver personalities love to plan and organize. In fact, they have probably already started planning a budget and they are not even in the "Creating a Budget" section of this working textbook yet. That is great! Those with a beaver personality toward money tend to be so focused on the creation process they never really get started implementing the budget. Alternatively, they implement the budget and make changes on a daily or weekly basis. Those who fall in this category need to 1) use the budget they created, 2) let their budget exist for a few months before making any changes, and 3) only make one or maybe two changes at a time rather than a complete overhaul of the budget.

Crocodile personalities are those who are unpredictable about money. Crocodiles are non-social, ruthless, sneaky, and focused only on survival. Crocodiles will do what needs to be done to survive. They do not have to work hard for their meals; they just need to be sneaky to catch their prey, for which they wait patiently. Once in the crocodile's jaws, the prey rarely has any chance of escape. This does not sound very appealing, but these are intelligent animals! Those with a crocodile personality tend to be introverts who spend time thinking about life. They keep to themselves, but they still have strong friendships. They also tend to find ways to cut corners, which is not always a negative thing. Cutting corners sometimes leads to more efficient ways of completing tasks. This personality type probably does not see a need to create and follow a budget. In fact, crocodile types most likely think it is a waste of time; this type prefers to live life as it comes. However, there are times when the crocodile regrets not planning because of missed opportunities. Crocodile types need to weigh the pros and cons of creating and following a budget. It will be difficult at first, but crocodile personalities can use their skills to fine tune an excellent budget. Financial success does not just happen; it is intentional.

What is your attitude toward money?

These animal personalities are a fun way to start thinking about how different personality types view money. Some people make a lot of money but do not know where all of it goes each month. They live paycheck to paycheck. Why? It is because of their attitude toward money. If you come to understand how you personally view money, then you can begin to discover your own strengths and weaknesses in financial matters. You can work to reinforce your strengths, learn how to overcome your weaknesses, and create a budget that will work for you.

EXERCISE 41

True or False:

1. True or False. Understanding one's attitude toward money is the first step to financial success.

2. True or False. Financial success is when a person becomes a millionaire.

3. True or False. Financial success is different for each and every person and is based on a person accomplishing their own financial goals.

4. True or False. Creating and following a reasonable budget can lead to increased opportunities and a higher probability of financial success.

Answer the Questions:

5. What is your personality/attitude toward money? ____________________

____

6. What are the strengths of your attitude toward money? ____________________

____

____

7. What are the weaknesses of your attitude toward money? ____________________

____

____

8. What changes can you implement now to improve your chances of creating and following a budget? ____________________

____

____

____

LESSON 42 - ALWAYS SEEKING FOR THE "GET RICH QUICK" SCHEME

Many people view financial success as earning a lot of money rather than accomplishing financial goals. High-income earners do not always have a lot of money. They may, however, have large amounts of debt causing their financial resources to quickly dwindle each month, leaving them with little extra. Conversely, there are many millionaires who are not high-income earners, but who have managed their money appropriately and saved to become financially successful. Financial success is not about how much money a person has, but about accomplishing financial goals. It is a reality that most people will not be millionaires in their lifetime; however, most can still be financially satisfied.

Many people look financially successful although they are under mountains of debt. The constant social pressure to be rich has led numerous people toward get rich schemes that are only scams. It is extremely rare that someone will "get rich quick." Financial wealth requires extreme and consistent effort for the majority of people. This effort includes planning, discipline, and hard work.

It is a myth that getting involved in a multi-level marketing company will be easy money. These companies are not "get rich quick" companies, but their marketing can sometimes make it seem like no effort is required to make a lot of money. For those who are top earners in these companies, they got there from a lot of planning, discipline, and hard work. They are also great at sales!

Except for inheritances, winning the lottery, winning big in a game show, or some other unusual and highly unlikely occurrence, most people will not get rich overnight. Yes, it may seem like that when a new company explodes in popularity overnight, but the founder of that company most likely had several failed ideas previously, and spent a lot of time planning, working, creating, and organizing.

'Get rich schemes' are SCHEMES!

Avoid them!

If an opportunity comes along that seems too good to be true and requires a substantial financial investment without quantified proof of stated revenues, it is probably a scam. Always research anything that appears too good to be true or too easy to earn money. Get advice from others before jumping into any situation which promises you can make an enormous amount of money overnight. Avoid opportunities that promise you will make money if you simply deposit a check from an unknown person or entity into your personal checking account in order to make money. If something looks shady, it probably is.

Those that devise "get rich quick schemes" know that people want to earn money as easily as possible. Some people are in far too much debt and are desperate to fix their financial problems. These schemes use the psychology of behavioral finance to prey on the emotions of people. Don't fall for it! Do the research, make sure a company is legitimate, and get sound advice from trustworthy people!

EXERCISE 42

True or False:

1. True of False. It's easy to get rich overnight.

2. True of False. If an opportunity to earn a lot of money quickly seems too good to be true, it probably is.

3. True of False. Financial success is different for everyone.

4. True of False. Most people become millionaire's in their lifetime.

5. True of False. Financial success takes planning, discipline, determination, and hard work.

6. True of False. Advice should be sought for any opportunity that seems like too good of a deal.

7. True of False. People who look rich most likely are rich.

8. True of False. Joining a multi-level marketing company is easy money.

9. True of False. It's incorrect that high-income earners are financial successful as many of them have a lot of debt.

10. True of False. Financial success isn't about how much money a person earns, but how well they manage their money.

SECTION 12 - CREATING A BUDGET

KEYWORDS

Deficit

Rolling budgets

LEARNING OBJECTIVES FOR SECTION 12

Upon successful completion of Section 12, you will be able to:

- Create a budget.
- Manage a budget.

LESSON 43 - BUDGETING BASICS

Creating and maintaining a budget has four steps: 1) list expected expenses and income for a given time period; 2) adjust expenses so there is not a deficit; 3) follow the created budget; and, 4) make adjustments to the budget as necessary. A **deficit** is when there is not enough income to pay for all of the expenses in a given time period. In personal finance, budgets are usually created on a monthly basis and are implemented as rolling budgets. In corporate finance, budgets are typically created on an annual basis. Some corporate budgets are a rolling "12-month" budget.

Rolling budgets usually do not have an ending date with a new budget created at the end of each period. They continue from month-to-month or year-to-year. However, instead of adjustments being made at the end of the time period created for the budget, adjustments are made as they come up to control spending and/or to allow for increases or decreases in income.
To begin a personal budget, a list of income and expenses needs to be completed. A simple budget format will usually look like this:

CATEGORY	MONTHLY BUDGETED AMOUNT
Income:	
Wages	
Interest Income	
Investments	
Other Income	
Total Income:	
Expenses:	
Total Expenses:	
Net Gain/Loss:	

Income categories are usually the same for most people; however, categories for expenses vary. When creating a budget, you should personalize the categories.

Loans are not considered income. A loan is borrowed money that has to be paid back. Unless the loan is a line of credit, the money from the loan goes directly to the purchase for which the loan was given, such as a car or house. Funds from a line of credit are available to a borrower but are also not considered income. These funds should not be included in the income section of a budget. This money is typically used for one-time purchases such as replacing a roof on a house.

Money from student loans are first paid directly to the college, and any excess money from the loan is given to the student or parent obtaining the loan. That money should be allocated toward other college expenses. Some budgets allow this money to be listed in the income category because the funds go toward living expenses, materials, books, etc., while in college. While it is stated as income in these situations, it is not considered income and should not be thought of as such. Income does not have to be paid back and loans do.

EXERCISE 43

List the four steps to creating and managing a budget in the correct order:

1. ______________________________
2. ______________________________
3. ______________________________
4. ______________________________

Multiple Choice Problems:

5. A deficit is:
    a. money that is owed within a given time period.
    b. when there is enough income to pay for all of the expenses in a given time period.
    c. when there is not enough income to pay for all of the expenses in a given time period.
    d. a shortfall in expenses in a given time period.

6. A budget that doesn't have an ending date and is adjusted as necessary is a:
    a. revolving budget.
    b. rolling budget.
    c. static budget.
    d. None of these.

7. The best way to start to define budget categories and their budgeted amounts is:
    a. to use the recent history of income and expenses.
    b. to make guesses based on what someone thinks will look good.
    c. to use already designed categories even if not needed.
    d. to lump everything into as few categories as possible.

8. Money from loans:
    a. is considered income.
    b. can be either income or not income.
    c. is not considered income.
    d. is considered an asset.

9. The expense categories:
    a. aren't really important.
    b. are not adjustable.
    c. are the same for each person.
    d. vary from person to person.

10. Money received from student loans:
    a. is income and always put in the income section to pay for college expenses.
    b. is not income, but sometimes put in the income section to pay for college expenses.
    c. both a and b.
    d. neither a or b.

LESSON 44 - CREATING A BUDGET ~ PART I

A monthly budget has been creted from the check register below. The first step in creating a budget is to list the income and then categorize the expenses. The best way to do this is by looking at the history of the actual money received and used.

Take a look at the register, then look at how money has been put into the budget. In this example, Pamela rents an apartment. The apartment company pays for water, sewer, and trash. Pamela is responsible for all other utiltities.

CATEGORY	MONTHLY BUDGETED AMOUNT	
Income:		
Wages	2,252.98	1
Interest Income	-	2
Investments	-	3
Other Income	-	4
Total Income:	2,252.98	5
Expenses:		
Savings	226.00	6
Charity	25.00	7
Rent/Mortgage	450.00	8
Renter's or Home Owner's Insurance	25.00	9
Auto Loan	225.00	10
Auto Insurance	125.00	11
Cell Phone Bill	95.27	12
Cable / Satellite / Internet	78.10	13
Electric Bill	53.76	14
Gas Bill	35.97	15
Trash Bill	-	16
Sewer & Water Bill	-	17
Food	169.53	18
Personal Maintenance	29.37	19
Entertainment	23.22	20
Eating Out	58.83	21
Clothes	132.73	22
Auto: Fuel	35.81	23
Auto: Repairs	400.00	24
Total Expenses	2,188.59	25
Net Gain/Loss:	64.39	26

DATE	REF	DESCRIPTION OF TRANSACTION	PAYMENT / DEBIT (-)	R	C	DEPOSIT / CREDIT (+)	BALANCE
		Beginning Balance					-
8/1/12	DEP	Paycheck				1,126.49	1,126.49
8/1/12	WD	Transfer to Savings	113.00				1,013.49
8/1/12	579	Apartments LLC Rent	450.00				563.49
8/2/12	580	Electric Company Electric bill	53.76				509.73
8/2/12	581	Gas Company Gas bill	35.97				473.76
8/4/12	DEBIT	Walmart Groceries	76.34				397.42
8/5/12	DEBIT	Conoco Auto: Fuel	35.81				361.61
8/10/12	DEBIT	Taco Bell Dining	10.29				351.32
8/10/12	582	Verizon Cell phone bill	95.27				256.05
8/10/12	583	Allstate Insurance Auto: Insurance	125.00				131.05
8/11/12	DEBIT	Applebees Dining with friends	23.76				107.29
8/11/12	DEBIT	Carmike Theaters Entertainment	10.75				96.54
8/13/12	EFT	United Way Charity	25.00				71.54
8/15/12	DEP	Paycheck				1126.49	1,198.03
8/15/12	WD	Transfer to Savings	113.00				1,085.03
8/17/12	584	Allstate Insurance Renter's insurance	25.00				1,060.03
8/20/12	DEBIT	Safeway Groceries	93.19				966.84
8/23/12	DEBIT	Ulta Personal Maintenance	29.37				937.47
8/24/12	DEBIT	Olive Garden Dining with friends	18.29				919.18
8/25/12	DEBIT	J. C. Penney Clothing	132.73				786.45
8/25/12	DEBIT	Cathy's Coffee Shop Dining with friends	6.49				779.96
8/28/12	EFT	Netflix Entertainment	12.47				767.49
8/28/12	EFT	ABC Financial Institution Auto: Loan Payment	225.00				542.49
8/30/12	DEBIT	Auto Repair Shop Auto: Repairs	400.00				142.49
8/30/12	585	Midco Internet & Cable	78.10				64.39

EXERCISE 44

Using the checkbook register on the next page, create a budget using the table on the next page.

CATEGORY	MONTHLY BUDGETED AMOUNT	
Income:		
Wages		1
Interest Income		2
Investments		3
Other Income		4
Total Income:		5
Expenses:		
Savings		6
Charity		7
Rent/Mortgage		8
Renter's or Home Owner's Insurance		9
Auto Loan		10
Auto Insurance		11
Cell Phone Bill		12
Cable / Satellite / Internet		13
Electric Bill		14
Gas Bill		15
Trash Bill		16
Sewer & Water Bill		17
Food		18
Personal Maintenance		19
Entertainment		20
Eating Out		21
Clothes		22
Auto: Fuel		23
Auto: Repairs		24
Total Expenses		25
Net Gain/Loss:		26

DATE	REF	DESCRIPTION OF TRANSACTION	PAYMENT / DEBIT (-)	R	c	DEPOSIT / CREDIT (+)	BALANCE
		Beginning Balance					-
8/1/12	DEP	Paycheck				900.00	900.00
8/1/12	WD	Transfer to Savings	90.00				810.00
8/1/12	579	Apartments LLC Rent	350.00				460.00
8/2/12	580	Electric Company Electric bill	46.29				413.71
8/2/12	581	Gas Company Gas bill	30.82				382.89
8/4/12	DEBIT	Walmart Groceries	56.71				326.18
8/5/12	DEBIT	Quik Trip Auto: Fuel	25.99				300.19
8/10/12	DEBIT	McDonalds Dining	9.77				290.42
8/10/12	582	AT & T Cell phone bill	73.15				217.27
8/10/12	583	Allstate Insurance Auto: Insurance	120.00				97.27
8/11/12	DEBIT	Chili's Dining with friends	23.76				73.51
8/11/12	DEBIT	Carmike Theaters Entertainment	9.75				63.76
8/13/12	EFT	United Way Charity	25.00				38.76
8/15/12	DEP	Paycheck				900.00	938.76
8/15/12	WD	Transfer to Savings	90.00				848.76
8/17/12	584	Allstate Insurance Renter's Insurance	25.00				823.76
8/20/12	DEBIT	Safeway Groceries	88.11				735.65
8/23/12	DEBIT	Ulta Personal Maintenance	20.37				715.28
8/24/12	DEBIT	Texas Roadhouse Dining with friends	19.76				695.52
8/25/12	DEBIT	Macy's Clothing	125.59				569.93
8/25/12	DEBIT	Johnny's Bakery Dining	9.46				560.47
8/28/12	EFT	Netflix Entertainment	12.47				548.00
8/28/12	EFT	ABC Financial Institution Auto: Loan Payment	195.00				353.00
8/30/12	DEBIT	Auto Repair Shop Auto: Repairs	225.00				128.00
8/30/12	585	Midco Internet & Cable	75.20				52.80

LESSON 45 - CREATING A BUDGET ~ PART II

Lesson 44 demonstrated how to create a new budget by using historical information from a check register. Doing this shows the individual's trends in spending. Does the budget show high expenditures in certain categories that can or should be decreased and low expenditures in categories that can or should be increased? For example, is a lot of money being spent on eating out or on clothing while no money is being put into savings? If the answer is yes, an adjustment should be to be made to those categories. Adjustments would also need to be made for any deficits.

Historical data for purchases made for daily living expenses using a credit card should be included in the budget. Daily living expenses would include groceries, personal maintenance items, cleaning supplies, dining, entertainment, clothing, gardening supplies, small auto supplies, and other like items. Basically, anything that is not a one-time purchase is a daily living expense. Putting money into a savings account will help with one-time, surprise purchases such as new tires or brakes on a car. Including these credit card purchases into the budget will most likely create a deficit. If this is the case, spending will have to be radically reduced and that can be a huge personal and emotional adjustment.

When using historical information to create a budget, you can create a budget based on historical spending and change how much is allocated in each category to budgeted expenses do not exceed expected income. Adjustments to various categories will probably need to be made. Once adjustments are made to the categories to ensure there is not a deficit and/or overspending in any of the categories, the next step is to use the budget by following it. After a few months, it is good to look at how the budget is working out.

Step 4 requires monitoring the actual against the budget. You might consider using money from one category to pay for expenses in another category. If this becomes consistent, the allocated amounts may need to be adjusted. Using Excel or the budgeting feature in Quicken allows for running totals in each category when entering money spent in each category. You will notice that some months all of the budgeting money in a particular category will be spent, overspent, or underspent. Using running totals helps with noticing trends in spending and/or weaknesses in the budget to make proper adjustments. A running total for each category will sometimes look like the spreadsheet illustration on the next page.

For example, notice that there are columns for January and February in the budget below. These show what was actually spent in each category for that month. The running total columns subtract the budgeted amount from what was spend for the month. Look at line 12 "Auto Gas" which shows in January the total spent on gasoline was $65.00, leaving a balance or running total of $10. In February for the same category, $70 was spent for gasoline. This left a running total or balance of $15.

Budgets help with accomplishing financial goals!

On the other hand, the Clothing category on line 24 shows a running total of $50 at the end of spending for January, but a deficit of $25 at the end of February. This category would not need to be adjusted because the person can adjust their spending.

Items like gas and electric are variable expenses. Remember, they must be paid each month, but the amount due changes based on consumption. For categories that vary month to month, it is best to take the average of the expenses over the past 12 months and use that number as the budgeted amount.

For a category in which the running total continues to increase each month, it may be good to decrease the budgeted amount for that category and allocate the difference to a category that is being overspent.

Additionally, if there is a one-time purchase item, such as an iPad, it can be included as a category and money allocated toward it each month. Once the dollar amount is reached, the item can be purchased. Then, a new goal can be set for any other large purchase you may want to make in the future.

CATEGORY	MONTHLY BUDGETED AMOUNT	January	Running Total	February	Running Total	
Income:						
Wages	1,800.00	1,800.00	-	1,800.00	-	1
Interest Income	-	-	-	-	-	2
Investments	-	-	-	-	-	3
Other Income	-	-	-	-	-	4
Total Income:	1,800.00	1,800.00	-	1,800.00	-	5
Expenses:						
Savings	200.00	200.00	-	200.00	-	6
Charity	100.00	100.00	-	100.00	-	7
Rent/Mortgage	350.00	350.00	-	350.00	-	8
Renter's or Home Owner Insurance	25.00	25.00	-	25.00	-	9
Auto Loan	195.00	195.00	-	195.00	-	10
Auto Insurance	120.00	120.00	-	120.00	-	11
Auto Gas	75.00	65.00	10.00	70.00	15.00	12
Auto Repair	50.00	-	50.00	26.00	74.00	13
Cell Phone Bill	73.15	73.15	-	73.15	-	14
Cable / Satelitte / Internet	75.20	75.20	-	75.20	-	15
Electric Bill	50.00	46.76	3.24	51.24	2.00	16
Gas Bill	35.00	36.76	(1.76)	33.33	(0.09)	17
Trash Bill	-	-	-	-	-	18
Sewer & Water Bill	-	-	-	-	-	19
Food	175.00	200.00	(25.00)	145.00	5.00	20
Personal Maintenance	25.00	20.00	5.00	15.00	15.00	21
Entertainment	75.00	65.00	10.00	60.00	25.00	22
Eating Out	75.00	80.00	(5.00)	65.00	5.00	23
Clothing	50.00	-	50.00	125.00	(25.00)	24
Miscellaneous	51.65	25.00	26.65	-	78.30	25
Total Expenses:	1,800.00	1,676.87	123.13	1,728.92	194.21	26
Net Gain/Loss:	-	123.13		71.08		27

EXERCISE 45

True or False:

1. True of False. Purchases for daily living expenses made with a credit card should be included in a budget.

2. True of False. Daily expenses include items that are purchased on a regular basis.

3. True of False. Making the adjustment to stop using a credit card for daily living expnses are both an emothional and personal adjustment.

4. True of False. The running total in a budget spreadsheet gives a clear picture of which categories show a continual deficit.

5. True of False. When saving for a large, one-time purchoase it is a good idea to create a separate category for that item.

6. True of False. Either an increase needs to be made for a category that is continually deficit or a decrease in spending for that category needs to be made.

7. True of False. The running total blance needs to be moved to the next month totals.

8. True of False. For expense categories where the blance continues to significantly increase, it is best to reduce the budgeted amount and apply that amount to a category that has a continual negative balance.

9. True of False. A rolling budget allows for continual adjustments as trends are noticed or circumstances change.

10. True of False. Showing the running totals for each category shows the strengths and weaknesses in spending and allows for more appropriate budget adjustments.

LESSON 46 - CREATING A BUDGET ~ PART III

Now, it is time for you to make your own budget. Since you are most likely a high school student completing this program, you may have many expenses paid on your behalf by someone else: a parent or guardian. Therefore, some research is required to complete your own budget.

First, talk with your parent or guardian and ask them to help you determine how much is spent for you each month. If that is not possible, do some research on the internet or ask a friend for help. The categories are going to vary from person to person. The following is a list of ideas to get you started.

Once you have determined your categories and a budgeted amount for each of them, enter this into the table in Exercise 46.

- Auto - Insurance
- Auto - Fuel
- Auto - Repairs/Maintenance
- Cell phone
- Clothing
- Entertainment
- Food - Groceries
- Food - Dining
- Internet
- Medical expenses
- Music lessons
- Personal maintenance
- Rent - Percentage of mortgage or average rental rates in your area.
- Renter's insurance - Average costs in your area.
- Savings - Put aside for you.
- School books and supplies.
- Sports activities
- Utilities - Percentage of gas, electric, trash, sewer, and water.
- Vacations
- Vision expenses - Glasses and/or contacts

EXERCISE 46

CATEGORY	MONTHLY BUDGETED AMOUNT
Income:	
Wages	
Interest Income	
Investments	
Other Income	
Total Income:	
Expenses:	
Total Expenses:	
Net Gain/Loss:	

1. Fill in category names for your expenses and their monthly cost.
2. Fill in the income you currently earn or would need to earn to pay for all of your expenses.
3. Do you earn enough to pay for all of your expenses? ____________________
4. How much do you need to earn to pay for all of your monthly expenses? ____________________
5. Which expenses could you decrease or budget less money for each month? ____________________
____
____
____
____
____
____
____
____
____
6. Are there expenses you were surprised to have? If so, what are they? ____________________
____
7. Are the expenses higher than you expected? If so, which ones? ____________________
____
____

FINAL COMPREHENSIVE EXAM

Multiple Choice Problems:

1. Money received from performing work or providing services is called:
    a. passive income.
    b. earned income.
    c. non-earned income.
    d. a gift-in-kind.

2. Companies typically refer to money that is earned as:
    a. revenues.
    b. income.
    c. earned income.
    d. passive income.

3. When a person receives an item in exchange for work performed or services given, it is called:
    a. revenues.
    b. earned income.
    c. passive income.
    d. gift-in-kind.

4. Fixed expenses:
    a. are costs that do change from month-to-month.
    b. are costs that do not change from month-to-month.
    c. are either a or b.
    d. are neither a or b.

5. Expenses that are not necessary to live are called:
    a. fixed expenses.
    b. variable expenses.
    c. discretionary expenses.
    d. mandatory expenses.

6. Expenses that are necessary each month, but change in cost based on consumption are:
    a. variable expenses.
    b. fixed expenses.
    c. mandatory expenses.
    d. discretionary expenses.

7. Money that is put aside for use at some point in the future is:
    a. for savings.
    b. used for monthly expenses.
    c. not necessary.
    d. None of the above.

8. Financial institutions have required memberships are known as:
    a. banks.
    b. credit unions.
    c. insurance companies.
    d. investment companies.

9. Financial institutions that do not require memberships are known as:
    a. credit unions.
    b. banks.
    c. all financial institutions require memberships.
    d. None of the above.

10. Money paid by a company to their shareholders is known as:
    a. an expense to the shareholder.
    b. a bonus to the shareholder.
    c. a dividend to the shareholder.
    d. a share to the shareholder.

11. The ending date of a loan is known as the:
    a. maturity date.
    b. start date.
    c. ending date.
    d. beginning date.

12. The penalty that is incurred when funds in CDs or IRAs are withdrawn before the allowed date is called:
    a. a penalty.
    b. a CD or IRA withdrawal penalty.
    c. a before maturity date penalty.
    d. an early withdrawal penalty.

13. Investments or assets that can be turned into cash quickly are considered to be:
    a. fast cash.
    b. liquid.
    c. quick cash.
    d. Any of the above.

14. Staggering the maturity dates of CDs is known as ________________:
    a. staggering.
    b. stacking.
    c. laddering.
    d. stepping.

15. Giving means:
    a. receiving something from someone after giving them something, too.
    b. giving something to someone else with an expectation of payment.
    c. giving something to someone else with an expectation of getting it back.
    d. freely giving something to someone else without an expectation of anything in return.

16. Creating a list of various deductions for a tax return to low one's tax liability is known as:
    a. itemizing deductions.
    b. listing deductions.
    c. cataloging deductions.
    d. citing deductions.

17. A tax liability is:
    a. money that is owned.
    b. money that is owed.
    c. is money that is owned or owed depending on the situation.
    d. None of these.

18. An item of value that is owned by an individual is:
    a. a current liability.
    b. a liability.
    c. an asset.
    d. an expense.

19. Personal net worth is calculated by:
    a. adding total liabilities to total assets.
    b. subtracting total liabilities from total assets.
    c. subtracting total assets from total liabilities.
    d. adding total assets to total monthly income.

20. Tangible items that are held for a long period of time and are not expected to be sold or converted to cash are:
    a. fixed liabilities.
    b. current assets.
    c. personal property.
    d. fixed assets.

21. Personal property:
    a. are assets that can be moved.
    b. are tangible items that are held for a long period of time and are not expected to be sold, or converted, to cash
    c. are liabilities that can be moved.
    d. None of the above.

22. Debts that are owed are:
    a. fixed assets.
    b. current assets.
    c. liabilities.
    d. Either a or b.

23. If total debts equal $225,000 and total assets equal $475,000, what is the debt Ratio:
    a. 40%
    b. 52%
    c. 47%
    d. 21%

24. Which of the following are examples of tangible assets for a business:
    a. Property, plant, and equipment
    b. Trademark
    c. Reputation
    d. Copyright

25. Which of the following is an example of an intangible asset:
    a. 2012 Ford Truck
    b. Boat
    c. Copyright for a book
    d. House

26. Which of the following is NOT a short-term liability:
    a. Auto loan due in six months.
    b. A house loan due in twenty years.
    c. A personal loan due in three months.
    d. A payday loan

27. Which department of the United States sets the minimum wage:
    a. United States Department of Wages
    b. United States Department of Salaries
    c. United States Department of Labor
    d. United States Department of Income

28. Which of the following Act enforces the minimum wage:
    a. Fair Labor Standards Act
    b. Fair Working Standards Act
    c. Sarbanes-Oxley Act of 2002
    d. Fair Labor Ethics Act

29. Which of the following defines gross wages:
    a. Gross wages are the monetary funds earned by an employer for work assigned.
    b. Gross wages are the benefits given to an employee by an employer.
    c. Gross wages are the monetary funds paid to employee after all deductions are subtracted.
    d. Gross wages are the monetary funds earned by an employee in exchange for work completed.

30. Which of the following is not an example of a retirement deduction:
    a. 401(k)
    b. Profit-sharing
    c. Child support
    d. IRA

31. Retirement plans can be all of the following except:
    a. Government sponsored
    b. Employer sponsored
    c. Personal
    d. All of the above are correct

32. Deductions can include which of the following:
    a. FICA
    b. State and local taxes
    c. Medicare tax
    d. All of the above

33. The opportunity cost of going to college fulltime is:
    a. fulltime income from working.
    b. sleeping in.
    c. not having to take classes and tests.
    d. None of these.

34. The opportunity cost of working fulltime is:
    a. less sleep.
    b. college degree to potentially increase income.
    c. more time with friends.
    d. None of these.

35. The Compound Interest formula is:
    a. PV = P(1 + r/n)Yn
    b. PV = FV(1 + r/n)Yn
    c. FV = P(1 + r/n)Yn
    d. P = FV (1 + r/n)Yn

36. The interest earned from and investment is called is:
    a. Interest rate income
    b. Investment income
    c. Speculation income
    d. None of these.

37. Which of the following is true:
    a. Incurring debt will make a person rich.
    b. Incurring debt will make life easier.
    c. Incurring is always necessary.
    d. Incurring debt should be used wisely as a financial tool.

38. $491.46 would be written as follows:
    a. Four hundred, ninetyone and 46/100 ------
    b. Four hundred and ninety-one and 46/100 -------
    c. Four hundred, ninety-one and 46/100 -------
    d. Four hundred, ninety-one and forty-six/100 ------

39. Money in accounts in banks and credit unions are insured:
    a. up to $300,000 for each depositor even if the institution isn't insured.
    b. up to $300,000 for each depositor per insured institution.
    c. up to $250,000 for each depositor even if the institution isn't insured.
    d. up to $250,000 for each depositor per insured institution.

40. A company that earns revenues through selling products and services and reinvests their earned revenues back into the company to benefit its members is known as:
    a. a for-profit company.
    b. a not-for-profit company.
    c. a non-profit company.
    d. a profit company.

41. What is the Federal withdrawal limit for savings accounts:
    a. Two withdrawals per month.
    b. Four withdrawals per month.
    c. Six withdrawals per month.
    d. There are no Federal withdrawals limits for savings accounts.

42. Transactions should be recorded into a register:
    a. It doesn't matter when
    b. Immediately
    c. Never
    d. Once a week

43. A type of stock where the shareholder usually does not have the voting rights is:
    a. Common stock
    b. Preferred stock
    c. Mutual stock
    d. Money market stock

44. A type of stock where the shareholder usually does have voting rights:
    a. Mutual stock
    b. Preferred stock
    c. Common stock
    d. Money market stock

45. The Five C's of Credit are:
    a. Character, capital, capacity, conditions, and collateral.
    b. Capital, capacity, conditions, collateral, and charm.
    c. Character, capability, capital, conditions, and collateral.
    d. Character, capital, capacity, circumstances, and collateral.

46. A credit report:
    a. is a report listing credit possibilities for a borrower.
    b. is a report listing the details of a person's credit history.
    c. is a report listing a person's work experience.
    d. None of the above.

47. The three most popular credit bureaus are:
    a. Experian, Equifax, and SubUnion.
    b. Experian, EquiNow, and TransUnion.
    c. Equifax, Experian, and TransUnion.
    d. Equifax, ExperFICO, and TransUnion.

48. The owner of a bond is a:
    a. debtholder.
    b. bondholder.
    c. bondsperson.
    d. bond debtor.

49. Each financial institution:
    a. uses the government standard interest rates for auto loans.
    b. copies their competitor's rates.
    c. has their own set of interest rates.
    d. uses the state interest rates published each morning.

50. Ken has the following monthly debt payments: $643 for mortgage, $95 for a student loan, $35 for a credit card, and will have a new loan payment of $206. His monthly gross income is $3,297. What is his DTI:
    a. 29.70%
    b. 28.10%
    c. 30.23%
    d. 31.94%

GLOSSARY

Accounts receivable - a long-term asset as a result of money owed to a company or individual that has not been received.

Amortization schedule - a table showing the payment schedule for a loan, including amounts paid to interest and principal for the given period and the resulting balance.

Amount owed - the amount of money owed to another person or company.

Appraisal - occurs when an expert gives an estimated value of property or goods.

Asset - an item of value that is owned by an individual or company.

Available balance - the difference between the credit limit and the outstanding balance.

Benefits - are considered part of the employee's pay package with an employer. They can include health and life insurance, paid time off, holiday pay, etc.

Bond rating agencies - agencies that rate bonds. Rating agencies include Standard & Poor's, Moody's, and Fitch.

Bonds - a type of marketable security.

Bond rating system - a grading system for bonds.

Bond yield - the difference of how much an investor paid for a bond and how much they made at maturity.

Borrower - an individual or company obtaining money from a lender.

Call option - when an individual or company has the right to buy a stock for a set price for a stated period of time.

Capacity - tells the lender if the borrower has enough income to pay the requested debt on time and continuously until the debt has been retired.

Capital - the money a person or company has invested in order to generate income.

Capital (borrower) - how much a borrower is putting down as a deposit toward a loan.

Capital appreciation - the difference between an investor's purchase price of an investment and the selling price of that same investment.

Capital gain - the increase in a capital asset. Investors don't realize the gain until the capital asset, such as securities, is sold.

Cash - money that is liquid.

Character - a borrower's willingness to repay their debts.

Closed-end loans - loans that have a maturity date and the paid down portion of the loan is not available to the borrower.

Co-borrower - a secondary borrower on a loan who has an equal obligation to pay the loan along with the primary borrower.

Collateral - the capital asset(s) that offers protection for the lender in case the borrower defaults on the loan.

Commissions - wages earned in addition to a base pay or without a base pay by meeting set goals, such as meeting sales goals for a month.

Commodities - basic goods, such as raw materials, that are used in the manufacturing of products

Common stocks - shares in a company. Owners are entitled to dividends and usually have voting rights.

Compound interest - accrues on both the principal and the interest earned in previous periods.

Conditions - applies to the current economy in the market where a borrower resides.

Contingent liabilities - obligations that may occur in the future.

Credit report - a report listing details of a person's credit history.

Credit mix - the combination of secured and unsecured loans incurred by an individual.

Current assets - see short-term assets.

Currents liabilities - see short-term liabilities.

Debt - money that is owed.

Debtholder - the owner of the bond.

Default - when an individual or company stops making their loan payments or becomes behind on their payments.

Deficit - when there is not enough income to pay for all of the expenses in a given time period.

Dependents - qualifying children or relatives as defined by the IRS.

Direct deposit - money electronically deposited directly into a checking or savings account.

Discretionary expenses - items purchased that do not have to be purchased in order to live.

Diversifying/diversification - to use a variety of savings and investment options with some being liquid and some harder to cash in.

Dividend - money paid by a company to their shareholders.

Dividend rate - total anticipated payment of dividends on an investment.

Early withdrawal period - period of time when funds cannot be withdrawn without losing the interest earned and paying penalties.

Earned income - money received from performing work or providing services.

Equity - the value in a property after all debts attached to the property have been subtracted.

Equity funds - investments in both U.S. and global stocks.

Established credit - the period of time an individual has credit.

Exempt wages –an employee who is considered exempt does not receive overtime pay. Exempt employees are usually at the management level.

Field of membership - qualifications that each person must meet in order to become a member of a particular credit union.

Five C's of Credit - character, capital, capacity, conditions, and collateral.

Fixed assets - tangible items that are held for a long period of time and are not expected to be sold, or converted, to cash.

Fixed expenses - are costs that do not change from month-to-month.

Fixed-income funds - corporate, municipal, and federal bonds.

Fixed interest rate - interest rate that stays exactly the same for an entire loan period.

For-profit - organizations focused on their operations making a profit.

Future value or FV - the value of something in the future.

Giving - freely giving something to someone

else without the expectation of anything in return.

Gross wage - the monetary funds earned by an employee in exchange for work completed.

Guarantors - an individual or company that signs on behalf of a borrower. They are not liable for the loan until the borrower defaults.

House poor - when an individual's monthly housing expenses exceeds their monthly income.

In-kind payment - a person receives an item in exchange for work performed such as receiving room and board for providing cleaning and childcare services.

Installment loans - loans with regular payments such as every month.

Intangible asset - something that cannot be seen or touch as it doesn't have a physical state.

Interest rates - the rate charged by creditors for loaning money to borrowers.

Internal Revenue Service (IRS) - governmental agency that collects taxes related to income.

Investment income - interest earned over time.

Investors - individuals or companies who put money into a product or service in hopes they will receive money in return that is greater than the initial investment that they made.

Investment income - interest earned from an investment over time.

Itemizing deductions - listing all allowable deductions in order to lower one's taxable income.

Laddering - opening several CDs with staggered maturity dates.

Lender - an individual, company, or financial institution that lends money to an individual or company.

Liability/Liabilities - debts that are owed.

Liquid - money that is easy to obtain quickly.

Liquidates - a company that goes out of business and sells all of its assets.

Living beyond one's means - individuals who use credit to spend more than have available.

Long-term assets - assets that are permanent in nature and will not be turned into cash within a year.

Long-term liabilities - a debt obligation that is due after a year or more.

Mailbox money - income earned on an investment without any active involvement.

Marketable securities - assets such as common stock and government bonds that can be easily converted to cash within a year.
Maturity date - the date at the end of the term.

Money manager - manages mutual funds at an investment firm or bank.

Money market funds - typically comprised of short-term debt securities.

Mutual fund - a marketable security comprised of a group of stocks, bonds, and other securities.

Mutual ownership model –savings and loans that can be owned by its depositors and borrowers.

Need - is something a person must have to live such as food, water, clothing, shelter, and human interaction.

Net income/profit - income after expenses.

Net wages - the remaining wages after all deductions are subtracted from an employee's gross wages.

New credit - a component of the FICO score system indicating new credit an individual has recently incurred.

Non-current liabilities - see long-term liabilities.

Non-passive income - income earned by investors who are actively involved in the management of a business.

Non-profit - organizations who earn revenues solely through charitable donations and/or grants. They are limited in how much net profit they can earn each year.

Not-for-profit - organizations that earn profits, but not for their owners/members, but to put back into their organizations to meet their goals.

Notes receivable - an asset in the form of a written promissory note held by a creditor which can be a financial institution or investor.

Open-end loan - a revolving loan with no maturity date.

Opportunity cost - that which is lost when one opportunity is chosen over an alternative opportunity.

Outstanding balance - the remaining obligation of a loan.

Overextended - when a person's income cannot meet, or pay for, their debt obligations.

Over-the-counter (OTC) - a bond that is traded using some other tool than one the stock exchanges.

Passive income - see unearned income.

Payday loans - an extremely short-term loan for a small amount of money.

Payment history - a component of the FICO score system indicating an individual's history of payments on loans and other credit items.

Personal Cash Flow Statement (PCFS) - measures all of a person's inflows (income) and outflows (expenses), which shows the net cash flow for a period of time, usually a month.

Personal Financial Statements - lists an individual's assets, liabilities, contingent liabilities, and net worth.

Personal income - money received for performing work, providing services, money received from investments, or through other types of incidences, such as child support.

Personal net worth - money owned after all liabilities are subtracted from all assets. It indicates the financial health of a person or company.

Personal property - something that can be moved from one place to another.

Preferred stocks - shares in a company that gives owners ownership of a company, but they don't usually have any voting rights.

Prepaid asset - when something is paid for before it becomes due.

Present value or PV - today's value of something.

Principal - the amount borrowed or owed on a loan.

Put option - when an individual or company has the right to sell a stock for a set price for a stated period of time.

Reconciliation - making adjustments of the differences between a Statement of Account balance and an account holder's balance in their checkbook register.

Revenue - typically used by companies on their financial statements.

Revolving loans - loans that do not have a maturity date where a borrower can continue to borrow on the loan up to the credit limit.

Risk adverse - an investor who doesn't want to lose any money or only lose very little money in an investment.

Rolling budgets - budgets that don't have an ending date. A new budget is created at the end of each period.

Savings - putting money aside for use at some point in the future.

Schedule of fees - fees that may be incurred with a financial institution can be for checking account, going under a required minimum balance, per check used, foreign ATM fees, etc.

Secured loan - a loan that has an asset pledged (collateral) against the loan.

Securities - an investment instrument purchased and sold in the financial market in order to make money by those who buy them.

Share account - a savings account held by a member at a credit union.

Shares - the portion of what is owned in a corporation or financial asset.

Shareholders - individuals or companies who invest and they hold shares, or ownership, in a company with stocks that they purchase.

Shareholders of a credit union - members of a credit union because they own shares in a credit union.

Short-term asset - an asset that will be sold, or converted to cash, within a year.

Short-term liabilities - debts or obligations due within one year.

Simple interest - interest earned by calculating it against the principal amount of a loan.

Source of cash - using credit cards as cash to make purchases and pay bills when no cash is available.

Stock option - when an individual or company has the right to buy (known as a call option) or sell (known as a put option) a stock for a set price for stated period of time.

Tangible assets –assets that have a physical state; they can be identified by touch.

Tax liability - how much tax is owed.

Time value of money (TVM) - money that is available today (present value) which has more value than the same amount of money in the future (future value) due to its earning potential.

Underwriting - a lender analyzes the strength and weaknesses of a borrower's credit history to determine if they should extend credit.

Unearned income - income that is received when work isn't performed and services are not provided.

Unsecured loans - loans that do not have any collateral protection.

Variable expenses - items that do not have to be purchased and typically varies with a person's income and/or activity.

Variable interest rate - varies over the period of the loan.

Want - a desire for something that is not needed. Sometimes these needs become confused with wants.

Made in United States
North Haven, CT
04 November 2026

21725025R00124